JOURNEY AWAY FROM TRAGEDY

JOURNEY AWAY FROM TRAGEDY

Foster Care and Spirit Guides

MARIE BOMAN

In Gratitude,
Jeannes M. Boman

Copyright © 2021 by Marie Boman.

Library of Congress Control Number:		2021921735
ISBN:	Hardcover	978-1-6641-9706-0
	Softcover	978-1-6641-9705-3
	eBook	978-1-6641-9704-6

All rights reserved. No part of this book may be reproduced or transmitted in any form or by any means, electronic or mechanical, including photocopying, recording, or by any information storage and retrieval system, without permission in writing from the copyright owner.

Any people depicted in stock imagery provided by Getty Images are models, and such images are being used for illustrative purposes only.
Certain stock imagery © Getty Images.

Print information available on the last page.

Rev. date: 10/25/2021

To order additional copies of this book, contact:
Xlibris
844-714-8691
www.Xlibris.com
Orders@Xlibris.com
832557

Contents

Introduction ix

Chapter 1 Back-to-Back Tragedies 1

Chapter 2 Family Move to California 22

Chapter 3 Path to Foster Care..56

Chapter 4 Marriage Proposal.. 120

DEDICATED TO...

my foster parents, my high school counselor, my spirit guides, and my friends who gave a young girl the courage to stand up for herself and the belief that she could do better and be better than her circumstances.

Introduction

I have often wondered why most of my early childhood memories are either the really good times or, mostly, the really bad times. Why can't I remember the average days, like being bored in school, playing in my bedroom, watching television at home with my sister, or playing outside with friends? Was it because my family did not live in one house long enough to build friendships? Maybe it was simply easier to remember the traumatic moments instead of the ordinary days. For many years, I wish I could forget the days that were filled with bad moments, but I have come to realize that those are the days that helped build my resilience and helped me overcome the tragic moments.

When I reflect on my childhood, living with my parents was like living in a pinball machine—looking at the seemingly protected silver balls from above bouncing from one spot to another, never settled, avoiding any circumstance that may cause a hit or a drop into a dark hole yet always emerging to face another game with different rules against the same opponent, never quite sure of the outcome of the game. My mother and I were the silver balls in the path of my father's verbal and physical attacks, the severity dependent on whether he was drunk or high on drugs.

Over the years, I told the story of my childhood to my husband and, after my divorce, to lovers who wanted to know everything about me and to friends who would ask where I had grown up. I came to realize that I told my story in a matter-of-fact manner, as if it had happened *around me* instead of *to me*:

- My father was in a penitentiary for grand larceny for the first two years of my life.

- My mother had a stroke that paralyzed the right side of her body when I was seven years old. She would suffer from depression for the rest of her life.
- When I was thirteen years old, I was sent to a foster home to live after testifying about the abuse inflicted upon me by my father in a closed family courtroom with a judge, a social worker, and my parents present.
- I lived in foster care until I got married one week before my seventeenth birthday.
- My mother successfully committed suicide when she was forty-one years old. I note "successfully" because she had attempted to take her life on two previous occasions.
- My father successfully committed suicide when he was thirty-nine years old, missing the one-year anniversary of my mother's death by nine days.

Friends would ask, "How did you turn out okay? How did you become the strong woman you are today?"

I would reply, "What was the alternative?"

I went about living life as it presented itself because I was a child who did not know there were options available other than living with my parents. I did not have the voice to say I was hurt except to my mother, who gave up trying to fight for my safety because she was busy defending herself. My mother and I both gave up. We were afraid of the repercussions we would receive from my father. We lived our lives trying to avoid him when he drank.

There was one memory I was unable to share openly with friends or lovers, the one truth that caused me the most shame, guilt, and embarrassment, a shame that physically manifested as a ball of negative energy filled with fear and anxiety stirring in the solar plexus of my body, causing me great anxiety whenever I would see a rape scene or sexual assault against a child or woman on the television. Decades would pass before I understood that the shame was not mine to bear, allowing me to speak my truth:

I was raped by my father when I was twelve years old.

I left this most tragic part of my childhood out of the narrative I was telling family, friends, and myself because I was too ashamed to say I had been raped by my father. I carried the guilt of feeling that I should have fought harder, screamed louder, that I should have told my mother the next morning before I had left for school. Instead, I chose to suppress this deeply painful event, convincing myself that it was a bad dream, a dream that would eventually fade away.

My contempt for my father increased with each beating he administered to my mother and me, causing me to wonder why my mother had not packed up our things to take us away from the abuse we both endured at his hands. As a preteen, I began to lose respect for my mother because she did not protect herself or her daughters. I could not understand why she continued to keep us in unsafe places that rarely felt like home. It would take thirty-five years of soul-searching before I understood my mother, a depressed, disabled, battered wife who must have felt that she had no choice other than to stay with her abusive husband.

I tell my story not to chronicle another horrifying crime perpetrated against a child by someone who was supposed to protect them but from the perspective of how I was able to overcome this tragedy by making a conscious choice to not be a victim of my circumstances, by paying attention to the signs presented to me, listening to the voices in my head, and listening to the people who appeared in my life during those times when I was in need of support and guidance to find a path away from more tragedy.

Guides

As a child, I never considered that there might be people outside our family who could help me. As children, we think living with our parents is our only option in life, so we focus on doing the things we are supposed to do—in my case, going to school, helping my disabled mother with household chores, caring for my younger sisters, trying to be invisible when my father was drunk or using drugs, just trying to live without conflict.

Fortunately, a complete stranger whom my father had brought into our home when I was twelve years old offered me an escape from my abusive circumstances, a chance for a better life. This stranger would be one of several people I would eventually come to believe were guides who would appear in my life at critical points to provide advice and direction toward alternate choices that I was not aware existed.

I would be exposed to the idea of spiritual guides during a session with a medium, a gift to me from my first boss, Joann T, when I was eighteen years old. Joann was a strong, intelligent, ambitious woman who would become one of the most important people in my life, professionally and personally. Coincidentally (I think not), Joann and my mother shared the exact same birth date: June 9, 1936!

Of course, at eighteen years of age, I had no expectations for my first session with a medium. For me, this session was for entertainment purposes only, an experience to expose my thought process to the idea that there was spiritual guidance beyond the limitations of what I was aware of at the time, which was limited to God and the church. I would keep an open mind and willingness to learn about spirits and energy beyond our worldly existence.

I cannot say that in all the moments when I would ask for help, I genuinely believed that my pleas would be answered because I had not yet embraced the practice of gratitude, much less the awareness, of spiritual guides. Then replies to my pleas for help began to reveal themselves over the years, guiding me away from harm, toward people who seemingly appeared in my life when I would cry for, pray for, and plead for help and guidance. As I healed and moved past my traumatic childhood, I would begin to recognize how fortunate I was to have been presented with kind, helpful individuals who would become known to me "at the right place at the right time" to provide me with the assistance, guidance, or opportunities I needed at critical junctures of my life.

I would eventually come to believe that my thoughts and internal pleas for help—crying for safety, pleading for relief from pain—manifested in the form of strangers who would seemingly appear when I was unsure of what to do to help myself. I believe that these strangers were brought to me by spiritual guides, the voices in our head that are often available to us if we can be still long enough to sense their presence and be willing to ask for their help and to listen to what is said when we feel the nudges in our bodies. Pay attention to that "being in the right place at the right time" feeling we have all experienced or when we are presented with seemingly coincidental or repetitive messages that appear in different forms, such as words from strangers or opportunities that seem to appear in those moments when you feel that no one sees you, that no one is listening to you. If you listen, you will know that you are not alone in your journey.

Guides are my purpose for telling my story because without them, I believe that I would not have found the path away from a tragic life. I would have been destined to mirror the behavior of my parents or land in even worse circumstances if these human guides and spirit guides had not appeared in my life at crucial moments to show me options beyond my circumstances.

The human guides showed me kindness and gave me advice, while the spirit guides/angels helped me sense, intuitively, if the physical guides were safe. The spirit guides made me aware that my light, my energy, was unique to me; I did not have to succumb to the darkness that surrounded me during my childhood. The nudges from spirits guided me toward opportunities and a better life that I could not have imagined existed for me if not for their intervention. These guides exist all around us and are here to help if we just take the time to listen.

Mother

I feel that I was born with a happy disposition, a trait I got from my mother. I see this disposition when I look at one of the few photos of me as a child, with my mother holding one-year-old me, smiling, with my finger in my mouth, sitting on my mother's lap, both of us looking toward the photographer. My mother's beautiful smile was outlined in red lipstick; I am guessing it is red lipstick even though the photo is black and white because I remember that most of her smiles were framed in red lipstick, highlighting her dark eyes, high cheekbones, and long wavy black hair. My mother's smile was like sunshine to me. Seeing her smile made me smile.

The purpose of this black-and-white photo was for our passport to travel to France to visit my father, who was stationed there with the U.S. Air Force. My mother must have been so excited for this trip to France and a chance to see where her paternal grandparents were born, to learn about her heritage, and to visit her husband. Sadly, for my mother, we never made it to France because my father went AWOL. He had been "dishonorably discharged" from the air force two months prior to our planned arrival in France and subsequently court-martialed for leaving his duty station. This would be the first of many times that my father would disappoint my mother and me.

My earliest childhood memories are when my mother and I lived with her parents in San Antonio, Texas, while my father was incarcerated. It would be decades before I would learn that we had to live with my grandparents because my father was serving a two-year prison term in Mississippi for grand larceny.

My grandparents called me Joannes Marie to avoid confusion when talking to my mother, whom I was named after. Eventually, all my family members would simply call my mother Joannes and me Marie. I remember my grandfather being playful with me, setting me on his lap most mornings at their small dining room table, me watching him dunk his hard toast into his cream-colored coffee that I would try to grab for a bite, making him laugh. I liked following my grandmother around the house, watching her cooking in the kitchen or gardening in the yard. I liked to play a game with them where I would try to sneak into the living room to grab a piece of hard candy from a candy dish that sat on their coffee table. I did not care about the candy as much as I wanted Grandma or Grandpa to catch me because it meant tickle time; my grandparents would reprimand me with tickles, telling me I was a naughty little girl. I felt so much love from my grandparents and my mother during this time, enough love to carry me through the impending chaos that would soon be my childhood.

My mother—the fourth child of seven children, five daughters and two sons—did not seem to be around a lot while we were living with her parents. I guess she was working or hanging out with her younger sisters, who, as teenagers, were still living at home with their parents at the time.

I wish my mother were in the few black-and-white photos she had taken of me on my third birthday—standing in her parents' driveway, dressed in a white puffy-sleeved dress with white socks and black shoes, shyly looking at the camera. My mother's big beautiful smile would be a reminder of this happy time when she was surrounded by the kindness and love of her parents. The photo would be a reminder of how our lives had been easier and happier when my father was absent. Of course, this is only conjecture on my part since the happiest days of my life would be those days when my father was not present. I really wish I knew how Mom was feeling about her future during this time.

I do not know how my mother could be optimistic about her future with my father, who, after receiving an undesirable discharge from the Air Force, was serving a two-year penitentiary sentence for burglarizing a gas station for money and tires, leaving her to care for their daughter, who would be four years old before he would see her.

Father

I gained an appreciation of all types of music from my father, who played the drums and constantly had loud music playing. I would develop traits of stubbornness and self-reliance because of my father's constant demeaning and/or challenge of almost every thought I would express.

My earliest memory of interacting with my father is when our family moved into a house in Dallas, Texas; I was five years old. He would often drop me off at school on his way to work, looking handsome with his brown wavy hair slicked back, dressed in a white shirt with a black tie and dark-colored pants cuffed just above his shined shoes, the two of us enjoying soul/R&B music that my father always had playing loudly on the radio during our morning drive.

I learned about my father's childhood fifteen years after his death when his brother contacted me, asking for information to help him do research on his family. I learned that my father had been abandoned by his nineteen-year-old father and fifteen-year-old mother when he was two years old, his parents putting him into foster care, where he lived until his grandmother found him when he was five years old.

My father quit high school in ninth grade for a "lack of interest," joining the Air Force in 1956, later getting his GED while in the air force. He would inherit his mother's alcoholism later, stating to a probation officer at a 1973 probation hearing, "I drink excessively. I drink all day every day. I have been drinking all my life." Alcoholism would be a part of who my father was until his death.

My father's mother died in 1972 at forty-eight years of age because of complications associated with alcoholism. I never met her. My father's father remarried once, to his second wife; they were together for over fifty years, and he lived for one hundred years, yet I never met him. I have never possessed a desire to refer to my father's parents as my grandparents because they were never a part of my life; nor were they involved in my father's life. I do not consider them to be my grandparents because they were never involved in the care or upbringing of my father; nor were they ever an influence in my life. I often wondered if my father may have had a chance to live a better life if he had received love and guidance from his parents.

Police records confirm that my father would continue to be irresponsible, getting arrested for carrying a concealed weapon as well as undergoing several arrests for drunk driving and the possession of dangerous drugs while living in Dallas and California.

I grew up thinking I wanted to be nothing like my father. He was my antagonist, my adversary, the person who harmed me the most. He seemed to challenge everything about me by constantly telling me I was "a stupid, immature kid who didn't know anything. You're too young and too stupid to know what is right." He may have been correct with his "too young" observation, but I convinced myself that I would prove him wrong about being stupid.

My goal was to become a smarter, kinder, successful person in spite of my father, not because of him. My father's constant ridicule would give me the voice that allowed me to speak up for myself. Maybe that was his parenting plan: badger me until I defended my position.

Finding out that my father had been abandoned by his parents and then placed into foster care allowed me to understand why he had become the person he was. He did not have the tools to be a good parent because he did not have parents who cared for him. He could have made better life choices, but he was, after all, only eighteen years old when I was born.

Decades would pass before I could find forgiveness in my heart for my father. Over time, I came to recognize that his doubt of my abilities only encouraged my determination to become a better person, to overcome and not succumb to the bad circumstances that were my childhood.

Parents

My parents came to California in February 1957. I was born on the Edwards Air Force Base in Pleasanton, California, in June. Their first marriage license was issued in the State of Mississippi, dated April 17, 1957. It would only be an assumption on my part that the Mississippi marriage was to make sure my mother was eligible for medical benefits and to make my birth legitimate.

My twenty-one-year-old mother was a tall five-foot-eleven slender beauty with eyes so dark, they looked black, matching her long wavy black hair, a stunning contrast to my eighteen-year-old father with a five-foot-nine frame, brown hair, and hazel eyes.

No one can tell me how my mother and father had met. I did not think to ask this question when they were alive because I did not care. I now regret not knowing. I would have asked my mother what it was about my father that had made her fall in love with him. Was it love, or did she marry him because she was pregnant with me? The answer is probably both.

I recall a story that my mother's eldest brother told me after her death about their shared love of dance. My mother and uncle would often go out dancing together on weekends, sometimes competing in local dance contests. I am sure they were a striking couple, my mother with the easy smile and sparkling eyes, dancing with her six-foot-three brother, having the time of their young lives.

I like to think that music was the catalyst that had brought my mother and father together while she was dancing with her brother at one of these clubs. My father played the drums and had a great appreciation for all genres of music, and my mother, enjoying the music while dancing with her brother, had probably caught the eye of my father, who happened to be in the same club—listening to music, wearing his air force uniform—and worked up the courage to approach my mother to ask her to dance.

Shortly after their meeting, Mom got pregnant with me. They got married.

My parents married a second time in Saint Mary's Church in San Antonio, Texas, on March 11, 1959. The witnesses (and only attendees at the ceremony) were my mother's parents, who wanted their third eldest daughter's marriage to be under the eyes of God at their Roman Catholic church.

My fondest memories of family time spent together usually involved loud music and laughter while dancing to James Brown (the "Godfather of Soul"), Aretha Franklin (the "Queen of Soul"), Little Richard, and Ray Charles, my father keeping beat on the dining room or coffee table with his drumsticks. He had learned to play the drums when he was a child but could not manage to hold onto his drum sets for very long in his adult life because his alcohol and drug addictions always left him short on money.

Mom was always willing to dance with my sister and me, twirling us around to the beat of the music or clapping with encouragement as we showed her our favorite dance moves. I still find myself wishing I could have seen my mother when she was single, dancing with her brother, happy and carefree.

Our neighbors often complained that the music coming from our house was too loud, asking my parents to turn down the volume; these requests only encouraged my father to turn the sound up louder. His pattern of not accepting responsibility for his actions and minimizing his involvement in bad behaviors would be his lifetime shortcoming.

Chapter One

Back-to-Back Tragedies

Dallas, Texas

My mother and I moved from her parents' home to government-subsidized housing, known as "the projects," on Pauline Avenue in the Dallas area with my father in 1961. This was the only place my parents were able to afford because of my father's recent release from prison.

My mother and father quickly rekindled their love for each other, exhibited by the birth of two more daughters, born barely fifteen months apart; my sister Faith was born in June, closely followed by the birth of my sister Janette, born in September of the following year. I was a big sister to two little babies before I was seven years old.

Both of my sisters were born in Parkland Hospital, the same hospital that President Kennedy was taken to on November 22, 1963. I was attending first grade at Stephen F. Austin Elementary School the day Kennedy was shot. I remember my teacher crying during class, telling us that school was being dismissed because the president was dead. I was too young to fully understand what was going on. It made me sad to see my teacher crying. I could not understand why she would be crying for someone she did not know. Of course, it all made sense to me years later in history class and in the movies about the assassination of President Kennedy.

Sadness and tears would fall upon our family in 1964 when an ambulance came to our house in the early morning hours on January 22 to take my youngest sister, Janette, away. When I came home from school that day, my parents told me Janette had died during the night while she was sleeping. I cried.

I asked, "Why did Janette die? She was only a baby."

My parents replied, "Sometimes babies get sick and just don't wake up."

In that moment, my six-year-old self accepted that answer, but later, I would wonder if older kids could also just not wake up one day too.

Janette disappeared from our lives too quickly after her arrival. I barely had a chance to smother her with big sister kisses.

Many times, I heard my parents tell friends and family members that Janette had died of sudden infant death syndrome (SIDS). I would later obtain Janette's death certificate, which shows that the immediate cause of death was enterocolitis because of pathogenic E. coli, a condition that can be transmitted from the mother's genital tract to the newborn during childbirth or from the mother's skin when breastfeeding.

My mother was overwhelmed with sadness after Janette's death. Her smile disappeared, along with her lively spirit. Our house was very still, filled with a strange quietness around all of us, largely because of the lack of my mother's presence as she mourned behind her closed bedroom door. Seemingly, she did not want Faith and me around, rarely leaving her bedroom to help me get ready for school or to make breakfast for her two remaining daughters.

I tried to stay close to my mother, giving her hugs and helping her around the house. I wanted her to know how much I loved her. I wanted to be a source of comfort for her, but something had changed. She was irritable, only interacting with me when she needed help with Faith. Seeing my mother not smiling or laughing, the sparkle in her eyes gone, made me sad. I missed my happy, loving mother.

My father masked his sadness with alcohol. He stopped getting home in time to have dinner with us, explaining that he had to work later because work was busy. The smell of liquor on his breath would eventually give him away. He was stopping at bars after work, coming home drunk most nights just as we were getting ready for bed, many times not coming home until after we were asleep.

It was a very unsettling time for me in our household because I was too young to understand my mother's sadness, too young to understand the sorrow that my parents were experiencing. My young mind did not have the capacity to understand that my sister was not coming back. Janette was gone forever. It seemed like my vibrant, happy mother was gone forever too.

As the months passed after my sister's death, arguments between my father and mother became nightly occurrences, always around dinnertime, when my father would take a bottle of liquor from the top of the refrigerator, my mother often walking behind him, pleading with him to sit down and have dinner before he drank more. He never listened to her request; he just yelled back that he was tired and just needed a drink to relax. My father's drinking never felt relaxing. A drink turned into multiple drinks. Multiple drinks meant that my parents would be fighting into the night on a nightly basis.

The more my father would drink, the more anxiety I would feel as the tempestuousness of my parents' relationship would erupt into another argument at the dinner table. These dinnertime arguments between my parents made me feel sad and, at times, scared when my mother would yell at my father about his drinking, attempting to pull the bottle of liquor away from him, only to have my father forcefully grab her arm to make her put the bottle back on the table. I would plead with my mother to please sit down and eat, to just let my father drink. I was worried that he was going to twist her arm to the point of breaking it.

I found myself wishing that my father would not come home for dinner. I wished he would go out to the bars after work so that my mother, sister, and I could have a peaceful evening, with Faith and me getting ready for bed, hopefully falling asleep before our father would come home.

My wish came true. Some weeks passed before my father took up his old habit of stopping at the bar instead of coming home after work. My mother, sister, and I happily got into the routine of enjoying quiet dinners without my father. I did not miss his presence at the dinner table, but I could tell that my mother was unhappy that he was not getting home until late into the evening, after my sister and I were already in bed, soundly sleeping.

Reflecting on this time, I realize that my mother had to feel so alone, left to care for her daughters by herself, knowing that her husband was getting drunk somewhere, anticipating a disruptive evening when he did finally get home.

The nights that my mother would stay up, waiting for my father to come home, would result in arguments, with her screaming at him for staying out so late. The arguments would escalate with, my father yelling obscenities at my mother, telling her to "sit down and shut the fuck up so you don't wake up the girls." At times, I thought I heard someone being slapped, followed by what I thought was furniture being dragged, crashing sounds, and more yelling. I was so afraid, but I had to comfort my little sister, who would often be awakened by the noise, I would take her out of her bed, bringing her to bed with me, holding her close as we both cried ourselves to sleep.

Sometimes I would work up enough nerve to open our bedroom door and yell at my parents, "Mommy, Daddy, please stop fighting! You are scaring us! Please go to bed so Faith and I can go to sleep."

Sometimes my pleas worked, and my parents would stop arguing and go to bed. Other times, they would yell at me, telling me to go back to bed and go to sleep. How selfish of them to think we could fall asleep with chaos happening just outside our bedroom door!

Anxiety began to overshadow our bedtime ritual of taking a bath before getting into our cozy pajamas, looking forward to a peaceful sleep. Anxiety was like a cloud hovering overhead, filled with our tears, waiting to burst. We were anticipating that our parents would be fighting as soon as our father got home, worried that their fighting might cause our mother to get hurt.

The arguments would continue, eventually escalating with the sounds of objects being thrown, chairs being pushed and knocked over, my father yelling at my mother, "Sit the fuck down before I throw you down!" Many times, he did throw my mother down. Many nights, we would hear her screaming as their arguments became more physical.

One night I was awakened by the sound of my father and mother screaming. At first, I thought I was dreaming because my father's screams did not sound like him. This scream was like a scream you would hear in a horror movie. When I realized that my mother was screaming for help, I jumped out of bed, opened my bedroom door, and ran toward the sound of my mother's voice, where I saw her in the kitchen, frantically filling a pot with water.

"Marie, help me! Help me get water to throw on your father. Your father is on fire!"

"On fire? Where is he on fire?"

"In our bedroom. Hurry!"

My mother and I ran from the kitchen, each of us holding a pot with water. As we ran down the hallway toward their bedroom, I could hear my father screaming in pain, screaming for us to hurry. As I was running toward my father's screams, all I could see were flames. As we got closer, I suddenly stopped. I was horrified to see my father sitting on the edge of their bed, his body in flames from his waist up to his neck. It appeared that everything but his legs was on fire.

I swear that my mother and I just stood still for a minute, not doing anything with the water, just standing there, staring at my father in flames. Were we in shock, or was my mother considering the consequence of just letting my father burn—letting him suffer, letting him feel the pain he had been inflicting on her? I too stopped, waiting for my mother's actions to show me what I should do.

Finally, we threw the pots of water on him, which doused the flames enough to allow my father to snap out of his panic and roll on the floor until all the flames were extinguished. There he lay, moaning on the bedroom floor, writhing in pain until the police and paramedics arrived. My father was loaded into the ambulance, my mother, sister, and I watching until the ambulance sped away to the hospital with sirens blasting.

My father suffered third-degree burns from his beltline to just below his neck. A few days passed before he returned home from the hospital, with his entire torso wrapped in white bandages. Eventually, the bandages came off, revealing what was now bright pink skin covered with milky white wounds and some areas that appeared to be black. It seemed like months passed, filled with the daily ritual of my mother applying ointments, my father swearing and sometimes yelling, my mother, often with tears in her eyes, getting some respite from the agony when my father would sleep for long periods during the healing process.

My father's torso would be severely scarred for the rest of his life from this accident. When I would see his scarred body, I would think that it still hurt, but he assured me that the pain was gone. Seeing my father comfortably walking around the house with his shirt off, comfortable in his own scarred skin, made me comfortable and less apprehensive about looking at him, knowing that he was not in pain.

Alcohol was the cause of my father's horrible accident. While in a drunken stupor, he decided to fill his Zippo lighter with lighter fluid, not realizing that he was also spraying lighter fluid onto his clothing. Once it was filled, he reassembled his lighter, took a cigarette out of his shirt pocket, and struck the Zippo to light the cigarette, which immediately set his lighter fluid–soaked shirt on fire. He was too drunk to think about dropping and rolling on the floor to extinguish the flames. My mother was too panicked to think about anything but getting water to douse the flames.

Although tragic, my father accidentally setting himself on fire had a positive side effect: he stopped drinking while he was healing. The affection between my parents at this time was unrecognizable to me. It made me happy to see them happy, working together as a team as they tended to my father's burn wounds, my mother carefully helping him clean his wounds, a painful process noted by the muffled screams and lots of swearing from my father.

Now that my father was no longer getting drunk, our dinners were peaceful and filled with conversation between my parents or between them and me, with me telling them about my day at school. My father was taking the time to sit with me to help me with my spelling words, while my mother cleaned up after dinner and got my sister ready for bed. Sweet dreams were assured when our sober father would kiss us good night and our mother would tuck us in with kisses, followed by a loving "Sweet dreams, girls. I will see you in the morning."

As I write about the aftermath of my father's tragic accident, I am struck by the strength of my then twenty-eight-year-old mother, who had already felt the loss of a daughter, followed by having to nurse her severely injured husband while taking care of two young daughters. That was quite the burden for a young woman who, not so long ago, was carefree, enjoying her single life out on the dance floor with her elder brother.

Dunaway Drive

Sometime after my father's accident, my parents began packing our belongings into boxes. When I asked them why they were packing our house up, they told me it was because we were going to be moving to a nicer house. This news excited me because I thought that a nicer house would mean that everything would be nicer.

A day came when our car trunk was packed with boxes and a large truck loaded with our furniture and more boxes followed us to a different neighborhood, where my father pulled our packed car up to a street curb, parking in front of a nice house with a large green lawn and big green bushes with white flowers under each window.

My mother and father exclaimed, "Welcome to our new home!"

I could not believe that we would be living in this big house, which looked much nicer than the house we had just moved from.

My excitement for Dunaway Drive was driven by my parents' smiles and enthusiasm as they raced with me to the front door, keys in hand. The unattractive concrete driveway that was our front yard at the other house was replaced with a grassy fenced-in lawn in the front and back yards. My sister and I would share a bedroom that was larger than the room we had shared in the previous house; this bedroom had windows looking out onto the big backyard, which beckoned us to play, but first, we had to unpack.

The abundance of safe outdoor space was a large playground for us to play with the new friends we would eventually make in our new neighborhood. This home was a new start for our family. My father was starting a new job with *Life Magazine* in advertisement. By all accounts, he had stopped his chaotic behavior to take care of his family.

This move was the beginning of the happiest period of my childhood memories living with my mother, father, and sister, all of us happy together, looking forward to new beginnings.

I loved spending time with my mother. She was elegant, with her long black hair cascading over her shoulders, her smile usually outlined by a hint of lipstick, unless she was going somewhere; then she would apply more red lipstick, which accentuated her dark sparkling eyes.

Most importantly, her fun personality had returned. She found ways to make us giggle as she went about the house, getting me ready for school and taking care of my sister. I liked helping my mother dress my little sister. We would have fun playing with Faith, making her laugh. I was happy to be mother's "little helper." We were a team. Her cheerfulness and beauty made me happy. I loved my mother. She was the most important person in my life.

For the first time, I felt proud of my father, seeing him dressed in a white shirt with a tie and black pants, looking handsome for his job at *Life Magazine*, dropping me off at elementary school most days on his way to work. His parting words were the same each time: "Marie, pay attention to your teacher today. I will see you at home tonight for dinner. I love you."

I remember feeling happy about dinnertimes on Dunaway Drive because my father had stopped going to bars to get drunk before coming home, eliminating my anxiety over whether or not my parents would be fighting before the night was over. My job was to set the table while my mother cooked dinner and Faith played nearby with her toys on the floor. My father would come home from work, still looking handsome in his work clothes, giving all of his "girls" a kiss hello before going to their bedroom to change out of his work clothes.

After dinner, while mother was doing dishes, my father would help me with my schoolwork, mostly spelling words, my favorite subject. Then my mother would get Faith ready for bed while I watched whatever my father was watching on the television before I too went to bed after good night kisses from both of my parents. Sweet dreams existed on Dunaway Drive.

Our new neighborhood was filled with lots of kids to play with in the front yards or in the flooded streets after torrential rainstorms, which seemed to appear often in Dallas. My parents were creating happy memories for their daughters, including one memorable Christmas when they made a five-foot Christmas tree using only colorful Sunday comics, with a couple of small presents underneath the tree for each of us. At the time, I was not aware that our homemade tree was a creative necessity because my parents did not have enough money for a real tree, but it did not matter because we were together and happy.

I felt loved and happy. Life was good on Dunaway Drive. This house, I would always remember as the one place that felt like home, the home with the best family memories of living with both of my parents present and happy at the same time. For a while we were a normal, happy family of four.

Then tragedy found us again on Dunaway Drive in the form of an ambulance with sirens on pulling up to our house. This time, the ambulance came for my mother. I was crying and screaming as the paramedics rolled my mother away on a bed with wheels.

"What's wrong with Mommy? I want to go with Mommy! I want to go with Mommy!"

I ran alongside the rolling bed, sobbing, waiting for my mother to say something, but she was not moving. Her eyes were closed.

My father dropped to his knees as he grabbed me, telling me to stop crying. "You are scaring your sister. Mommy will be okay."

Daddy did not look like he thought Mommy would be okay. I was scared. I thought she was dead.

I watched as the ambulance sped away, with its screaming sirens and red flashing lights disappearing, with my mother inside. I stood on our lawn sobbing, not moving until I could no longer see the red lights of the ambulance. My sister did not come back when the ambulance had taken her away; I did not think that my mother would be coming back either.

My mother would not be okay. She had a stroke from a blood clot on her brain, leaving her paralyzed on the right side of her body. It seemed like an awfully long time before she came home from the hospital. When my mother did return home, she no longer smiled. Her sparkling eyes were replaced with a sad, tired face that drooped on the right side. When she would try to speak, I could not understand the words she was saying as she walked toward me, dragging her right leg behind her, trying to lift her right arm with her left hand to hug me.

I can still see her trying so hard to lift that dead arm, to reach out to me while I stood still, crying. "Mommy, what happened? How did you get hurt? Are you okay?"

The cause cited for my mother's stroke was from taking the birth control pill, which had higher levels of estrogen and progestin from 1960 to the 1990s. This high-dose combination birth control pill would increase stroke risk in women nearly threefold. However, I cannot help but wonder if my mother's stroke was caused by the stress of having two babies within fifteen months of each other, followed by the death of her youngest daughter and the added stress of my father's continued drinking problems.

My mother was only home for a short time before she went away for a brief period to receive intense physical therapy as well as treatment for depression. One of my mother's relatives, along with her two young children, came to live with us on Dunaway Drive while my mother was away. I did not like having strangers invading our family, and I did not understand why my father could not take care of us. I told my father that I would help him take care of my sister. I told him that we didn't need anyone else in our house.

"We can take care of ourselves."

"Marie, you are too young to take care of your sister by yourself. You have to go to school, and I have to go to work."

I was angry when I realized that this woman and her kids were going to live with us. I was too sad to have strangers living in our house, sharing my bedroom, playing with my little sister, having fun. My mother was extremely sick; this was not a time for visitors.

Dunaway Drive became a lonely place for me without my mother. This house no longer felt like home; without my mother, Dunaway Drive was simply a house filled with strangers and turmoil. It was not the home I loved, filled with my mother's beauty, smiles, and loving personality.

My father started to drink regularly again after my mother's stroke, yet he did not seem as angry as he had been on previous drinking binges. Over time, I would learn that alcohol was the catalyst for my father's personality. Depending on how much he drank, he could be charming, funny, angry, scary, and eventually violent, depending on the status of his working life and the people with whom he surrounded himself. He seemed to be on his best behavior around this relative who had moved in with us. I had a sense that he had to somewhat control his drinking to avoid any angry outbursts if he wanted her to continue to help him with his daughters and maintain the household until my mother was able to come home for good.

I was slowly getting used to having this stranger around to help. She was, after all, a nice person, and her young children were good playmates for my sister and company for me to take my mind away from missing my mother. I helped whenever she asked, but I also kept emotional distance because she was not my mother. I did not want my mother to feel that another woman was replacing her in my heart. It was important to me that my mother knew that I missed her, I loved her, and I would be there for her when she needed me. During my mother's absences, I would concentrate on being a good big sister to Faith and a good student to make my mother proud of me when she returned home for good, healed and smiling.

Then life got really confusing for me. One morning, while getting ready for school, I walked into my parents' bedroom to ask my father if he was going to drive me to school. When I opened the bedroom door, I saw the woman who had moved in to help take care of us in my parents' bed with my father. They were making moaning sounds. I suddenly realized that they were both naked. All I could think was *Why? Why is my father in bed with this woman?*

I screamed, "DADDY, WHY ARE THE TWO OF YOU IN YOUR AND MOMMY'S BED?"

My startled father yelled at me. "Close that door! Why aren't you getting ready for school? Why did you open my bedroom door?"

I could feel the tears welling in my eyes as I realized that my father had been kissing this woman. I ran down the hallway toward the bathroom, crying.

My father yelled, "Marie, come back here!"

I locked myself in the bathroom, sobbing as I took a shower, wanting to get ready for school as quickly as possible, hoping that I could get dressed, get out of the house, and run to school without having to look at my father. I was furious and hurt, knowing that what I had just witnessed would hurt my mother too.

When I was finished taking a shower, I wrote, "HORE! SHE IS A HORE!" on the steamed bathroom mirror. Wrapped in a bath towel, I opened the bathroom door to see my father waiting for me in the hallway.

He began screaming at me for opening the bedroom door. "YOU HAD NO FUCKING BUSINESS OPENING THE DOOR TO MY BEDROOM! WHAT HAPPENS IN MY BEDROOM IS NONE OF YOUR FUCKING BUSINESS!"

Through sobs, I screamed, "IT'S NOT *YOUR* BEDROOM! IT'S MOM'S BEDROOM TOO!"

Then he saw the words I had written on the bathroom mirror. "YOU ARE SO FUCKING STUPID! YOU DON'T EVEN KNOW HOW TO SPELL CORRECTLY! YOU MEANT TO WRITE W-H-O-R-E!"

"I DON'T CARE IF I DON'T KNOW HOW TO SPELL 'WHORE'! SHE IS A WHORE, AND I HATE BOTH OF YOU!"

I tried to run to my bedroom, but my father caught up to me, grabbing my arm before I could get away. He struggled to hold me while trying to remove the belt from his pants. The bath towel fell from my body, leaving my bare skin exposed for the lashings that hit my bare legs and buttocks.

Through tears and screams, I begged my father to stop. "I'm sorry. I'm sorry." I was not sorry. I just wanted the pain to stop.

I do not remember if my father lost his grip on me or if the woman was able to make him stop, but I got away and ran to my bedroom, where I threw myself on my bed, sobbing. Then she came into my room and tried to sit on my bed to talk to me, to calm me down.

I told her to get away from me. "I don't want you to talk to me ever again. I hate you. I want my mother."

I did not want to come out of my room, but I also did not want to be in the house with my father and this woman. My dilemma was solved for me when my father, standing at my bedroom door, yelled at me to "get dressed! You are going to school today."

I could not stop crying as I searched through my clothes for long pants to wear to hide the red welts on my legs left by the belt marks. Even though

I wanted to go to school to get out of the house, I was worried because I was so angry, my anger making me cry even more. I just could not stop crying.

The thought of staying in this house with this woman and my father, acting like my mother did not exist, made me want to run away. I could not stand to look at either of them. They made me sick to my stomach. I had to get out of the house.

I wanted to get as far away from my father as possible, but he had to drive me to school, so I sat in the backseat so I would not have to look at his face. I concentrated on not crying as my father continued to lecture me about respecting his privacy. I had so many words in my head that I wanted to scream at my father, but I just stared out the car window, trying to concentrate on not crying. I felt power in my silence because I did not have any words to say to my father that would express my total contempt for him. I also did not want to show up at school looking like I had been crying.

I have always felt that the intensity of the beating my father had delivered was not because I had opened the bedroom door, not because I had misspelled "whore." It was because I had caught my father in the act of doing something he should not have been doing. He knew that I knew he was doing something wrong.

This incident would be the precursor to my behavior change toward my father. I lost respect for him. He had betrayed Mother, and he had betrayed his daughters. I felt that his actions with this woman meant that he did not love us and that his family was no longer important to him.

I still find some humor at the idea of my father beating me, a child, because I did not know how to spell the word "whore" correctly. My father's lack of accepting responsibility for his actions, along with his rationalization for making bad decisions, would be part of who he was for his entire life.

Dunaway Drive was no longer a happy place for me. I could not stand having this woman in our house. Looking at her and my father disgusted me. She tried to explain that I was too young to understand what adult relationships were about. She told me that she loved me, my sister, and my mother very much. I told her that she was a liar and that I did not want "to talk to her ever!" Our happy home became a place where I avoided her and my father as much as possible by staying in my room while also making sure my father did not hear me when I would lash out at her when she would try to talk to me. Otherwise, his belt would come off from around his waist to give me another whipping.

I was so angry and unhappy. I resented having to sit with my father and these strangers at mealtimes, pretending we were a normal family. There was nothing that felt normal to me anymore in our home. I missed my mother. I needed to spend time with her. I wanted her to be home for good.

When my mother finally did come home, her ability to speak was better, making it easier to understand her when she spoke.

"Come here, Marie. I've missed you. I love you."

Her right leg was still dragging behind her, her crooked smile lighting up her face to accent the sparkle in her eyes. She was slowly returning to herself. The physical therapy had made her left arm stronger, allowing her to hurl her right arm up onto my shoulders and hug me with both arms.

My sadness for her injuries was somewhat soothed by the return of her spirit. I could see her spark strengthening, yet her body got tired quickly, causing her to stay in her bedroom for what seemed like most of the hours in the day. I would sneak in to see her when I got home from school, but she would be asleep or tell me to go away. I would feel hurt and sad when she would tell me to go away. At the time, I did not understand that it was depression that made her say these unkind words to me. Still, I was glad that my beautiful mother was home.

Shortly after my mother had returned home, my sister left with the relative and her kids to live with them until my mother regained her strength. I got to stay home because my father thought eight-year-old me could help him take care of my mother. My parents also wanted me to continue going to the same school.

Time on Dunaway Drive was quiet and lonely for me, with my mother spending most of the time in her bedroom, rarely coming out to sit on the couch with me to watch television or ask me about my day at school.

I would help my mother make dinner to have ready when my father got home from work. The three of us would sit at the table, with me talking about my day at school, my mother listening and asking questions but not with the same energy or enthusiasm that she had before her stroke. It made me sad to see my mother looking so unhappy. She was not smiling, and the sparkle I so enjoyed seeing in her eyes when she smiled was disappearing again.

It was not long after my sister's departure that my father returned to his bad habit of drinking heavily. His habitual drinking would affect his ability to show up for work and would eventually be the cause for him to be fired from his job at *Life Magazine*. Probation records show that he was arrested several times in Dallas on drunk driving charges and the possession of "dangerous drugs." Fortunately for my father, these charges were settled by paying fines.

I would often see my father stumbling around the house as if he had no sense of where he was, many times my mother following behind him, trying to grab the booze bottle from him, screaming at him to stop his drinking. Of course, it was easy for my father to simply push my mother away with her disadvantage of only one good arm to grab him with and one paralyzed leg slowing her down as she would try to chase him around the house.

Through tears, I would ask my mother to please sit down. "Just let Daddy drink. He's not going to stop drinking!"

Many times, my father would be laughing at my mother when she was trying to catch him, like it was some kind of game they were playing. I was so afraid that my mother was going to hurt herself from chasing after my father, who did not seem to care about her safety.

My mother screaming at my father and my father screaming back, yelling obscenities, would become the new normal in our household. There was rarely a day when my parents were not screaming at each other. The screaming eventually escalated to my mother trying to scratch at my father's arms and face or trying to pull his hair, only to be swatted away by him. I would cry and plead with them to stop fighting. When they did listen to me, it seemed like only a brief respite, which would continue again depending on how much my father would drink every night.

My father often drank so much, making him incoherent and unaware of his surroundings. Once, he removed a plate of leftover rotting chicken from the top of our refrigerator that was infested with maggots. I was walking toward him to get something out of the refrigerator when I saw white bugs crawling on the chicken.

I yelled, *"Daddy, why are you eating chicken with bugs?"*

It took a moment for his drunken brain to realize what I was telling him. He just stared at the plate for several moments until he realized that he was, in fact, eating maggots.

He threw the plate down, screaming, "Those aren't bugs! Those are fucking maggots! I was eating maggots!"

I had to turn away for a moment to hide my laughter. I thought it was funny that he was so drunk that he did not know he was eating food covered in maggots. I also felt a sense of satisfaction that he did eat some of the chicken before realizing it was rotten with maggots. He deserved to feel discomfort since being uncomfortable was how he made me feel in our home every time he was drunk.

After losing his job, my father spent his days hanging out at bars, drinking and playing pool for money, sometimes taking me with him. My mother was home, but she continued to spend most of her time in the bedroom. I got comfortable knowing she was in the house, even though I was not allowed to interact with her until she came out of her bedroom. I would spend my time watching television or occasionally going outside to play with my friends in the neighborhood.

I do not know what prompted my father's decision to start taking me with him to the bars he frequented. I was content to be home watching television or doing schoolwork, comfortable knowing my mother was close by if I needed her.

When I asked him why I had to go to the bars with him, he said, "To keep me company, Marie. Don't you like keeping Daddy company?"

"I can keep you company at home with Mommy," I said.

There was nothing from him acknowledging my response, confirming what I already knew—his drinking was more important to him than how I felt about being dragged into bars.

Being with my father when he was drunk was scary, starting with the ride to the bar, with me in the back seat of the car, begging my father to slow down as he swerved in and out of his lane, driving very fast. I would often cover my eyes with my hands, crying and yelling in frustration, "Daddy, please slow down! I am scared! You are driving too fast. You are swerving too close to the cars. Please slow down!" My pleas were ignored.

One day Daddy's luck ran out when he sideswiped a car in the lane next to us. I was worried when he had to pull over to speak with the man whose car he had damaged. I was worried that the man would be angry and might fight with my father. I do not recall hearing the conversation between my father and the other male driver, but my father did point to me in the car a couple of times when he was talking to the other driver, maybe apologizing to the man for hitting his car because he was distracted by me begging him to stop. All I know is that my father handed the man some money with a piece of paper; then we continued our drive to the bar.

I blame my father's bad driving for my lifelong fear of being a passenger; no matter how good the driver, I am always nervous when I am not driving. I even get nervous when I am driving, always anticipating a car getting too close, whether it be the side or the back of the car. I need to maintain lots of space between my car and the cars around me.

I continued pleading with my father to let me stay home, but he would not listen. Instead, he would take me inside bars with him, where I would sit at a booth that was not too close to the front door but close enough for my father to see me from the pool table where he was at, hustling games for money.

My father would tell me to stay put and do my homework. He would occasionally look over at me and give me a thumbs-up, his way of asking if I was okay. Sometimes I would show him a thumbs-down, but it did not matter to him; he was not going to take me home until he was ready to leave the bar.

In the beginning, I was entertained with people watching, identifying the people who, like my father, drank a lot. I was making bets with myself on who I thought would be drunk first, who I thought had kids like my father, and why no one else was bringing children to hang out in the bars.

It was almost impossible to do my homework in the back of a dark bar that smelled like old beer and had damp, sticky floors and loud music playing from a jukebox. Most of the time, I would just sit there, bored, watching my father play pool, trying to avoid making eye contact with anyone in the bar. I appreciated that the cocktail waitresses were nice to me, bringing me sodas and asking if I was okay. I was not okay. I just learned to say I was fine so that people would leave me alone. I wanted to be at home, not in a bar.

On one of these field trips to the bar, a man sat down next to me in the booth and started to ask me questions: "How old are you? Where is your mother? Is that your father over there playing pool?" I began feeling uncomfortable; this man was sitting too close to me, and I did not feel like talking to him. I cried out for my father, who immediately ran toward me, holding a pool stick above his head like he was going to hit the man.

He pulled the man out of the booth, yelling at him, "Don't you fucking talk to my daughter! I will fucking kill you with this pool stick if you even look at her again!"

The man walked away. I was relieved that my father did not have to kill him.

My father sat down next to me in the booth, putting his arm around me, looking into my eyes. "Are you okay, Marie? Did that man touch you or just scare you?"

"I'm okay, Daddy. That man didn't touch me. He just scared me. Will you please take me home now?"

In that moment, I felt admiration for my father, my protector. I knew he would take care of me, keep me from harm. Later in life, I would recognize this incident as another selfish, irresponsible decision made by my father, yet in that moment, I felt that he loved and cared for me. I could feel safe amidst the chaos knowing he had one eye on me and one eye on the pool table as he hustled for money.

The incident with the man at the bar got me a reprieve from future trips to the bar with my father. He decided to let me stay home, trusting me to do my homework and not bother my mother. He did not want me going outside to play with the neighborhood kids unless he was home, which made me feel lonely and sometimes bored, but I preferred being in the safety of our house instead of sitting in a dark, stinky, loud bar filled with strangers.

My quiet time at home was short-lived when my mother had to leave home again to go to a medical facility to get treatment for her depression and suicidal thoughts. My father thought I would be safer with him than being at home by myself, so my trips to the bar with him resumed. This time, he asked the cocktail waitresses if I could sit at the bar counter. Of course, they let me; what choice did they have? My father was a regular paying customer with a kid who needed a place to get her homework done. I guess there were no laws against minors sitting at bars in 1966.

St. Joseph's Home for Girls

One day my father sat me down to tell me, "Mommy is going to be gone a little longer to keep getting help so she can get better, and I need to go back to work to pay the bills so we can stay in this house. You are going to go to a school where you will stay until Mommy comes home."

I was nine years old when my father dropped me off at St. Joseph's Home for Girls, a Catholic school. I thought I was simply being dropped off at a new school for the day. It was not until I saw that my father handed a small suitcase to a nun that I realized what he had meant when he told me I was going to "stay" at a school. I felt tears begin to well in my eyes.

My father got down on his knees. Looking me in the eye, he said, "Marie, you're going to go to school and live here for a little while until Mommy can come home."

I started to sob. "But why? Why can't I stay at home with you?"

"Because, honey, I need to get a job and work so that we have a nice home for you and your mother to come home to when she's better."

"When will I see you and Mom again?"

"Soon, honey, soon. You just focus on your schoolwork, do what the nuns tell you, and I will come get you as soon as your mom is better."

I remember feeling like I was being punished for something I did not know I had done. I could not understand why I was being removed from our home when I had done nothing wrong. I did not know where my mother was. I did not know why my father could not take care of me. I did not want to live with anyone but my family. I was confused, hurt, and lonely.

I could not help feeling that I did something wrong to be abandoned by my family. No one came to visit me during my time at St. Joseph's, not my father or my mother. No one visited or called me during the six months I lived with the nuns.

I entered St. Joseph's feeling scared, lonely, and unsure. I had no idea what to expect as a stern-looking nun took my hand and my suitcase of clothes, telling me she would walk me to the dormitory where I would meet the "other girls." I tried very hard not to cry as I walked hand in hand with the sister down the long quiet hallway with shiny, clean floors and pictures of angels on the walls because I did not want the "other girls" whom I had not even met yet to see me crying. The sister tried to assure me that I had nothing to be afraid of, that the girls would help me put my things away and show me around the dormitory.

Too many years have passed for me to recall the names of any of the girls I became friends with at St. Joseph's, but the sister was right. All the girls I met during my time at St. Joseph's were nice, helpful, kind, and fun schoolmates and roommates.

My time at St Joseph's settled into a nice daily routine of getting ready for school, dressing in the school-provided maroon sleeveless plaid dress with a short puffy-sleeved white blouse underneath, completing our daily uniform, and then going to eat breakfast in the cafeteria before heading off to the classrooms to study Christian doctrine, reading, English, spelling, mathematics, handwriting, and history, taught by the sisters in their full habit uniforms. My report card shows that I was an "above average" student in every subject but Christian doctrine and history. Reading was becoming my favorite subject.

After classes, we did homework and reading, followed by some playtime outside or board games in the common area before dinnertime. Weekends were for chores, followed by fun activities that included listening to music, playing kickball on the playground, or simply hanging out with the other girls, talking and laughing. I slept in a room with other girls my age whom I considered my friends. Having friends made it easier to be away from home. The loneliness that had overwhelmed me when I entered St. Joseph's was slowly disappearing.

Waking up early on weekends to do difficult chores, like waxing long hallways with a buffing machine, would be one of my least favorite activities while at St. Joseph's. I recall that the floor buffer was bigger and taller than I was, dragging me up and down the long hallway. I was not controlling it; it was controlling me, getting me in trouble with the sisters, who would reprimand me for banging the buffer into the walls. I would exclaim that I was not strong enough to control the floor buffer, but I received no sympathy, just a stern look, followed by a strong rebuke: "You will get the job done if you expect to participate in tomorrow's field trip to see a movie." I did get the job done as best as I could, missing some spots along the way but shining enough of the area to be released from the task and rewarded with movie night.

Movie night began with our group of about twenty excited girls boarding the school's bus for the trip to the movie theater. It was a big deal to leave the school grounds for a movie. This was my first school field trip and my first time seeing a movie on the big theater screen.

What a wonderful movie it would be—*The Sound of Music*, the real-life story about a family of singers who lived in a beautiful mountain town and had a happy, carefree governess who happily sang beautiful songs to lift their spirits! The scenery was thrilling, and the family was perfect. I would memorize the songs "The Sound of Music," "Do-Re-Mi," and "My Favorite Things" to sing along with the other girls for weeks after seeing the movie. Sitting in a movie theater for the first time, watching *The Sound of Music* on a big theater screen, surrounded by school girlfriends, would be a fond memory that stayed with me for years, often reminding me to sing these songs, which could easily lift my spirits.

Having a regular schedule at St. Joseph's for my first semester of fourth grade, even the chores, taught me discipline and gave me a sense of accomplishment that I had yet to experience while living with my parents. Even though I missed my family and sometimes wondered if they were actually coming back to take me home, I am grateful for the three months I spent at St. Joseph's, where I learned the value of working hard and the rewards of doing a job well.

Life after St. Joseph's

When it was time for me to leave St. Joseph's, I was taken to the front office, where my father was waiting to pick me up. I was disappointed to see that he was standing alone in the office; my mother was not with him. I had hoped she would be out of the hospital, feeling well enough to come and pick me up.

As we walked toward the front door, my father said, "I have a surprise for you in the car."

"A surprise? What is it?"

"You'll see when you get to the car."

I started walking a little faster, anticipating that something good was waiting for me. I was not disappointed. There, standing outside of the car, was my beautiful, smiling mother.

"Marie, come to me. Come give me a hug!"

I ran, yelling, "Mommy! Mommy, you're back!"

I threw myself at her, crying tears of joy as she hugged me tight into her body with her strong left arm. My mother had returned. This was the best day ever!

I could barely contain myself during the ride home. I was so happy to see my mother and my father seemingly sober and calm, both asking me questions about how I liked going to school at St. Joseph's. I could not wait to get into the house to unpack my things in my bedroom and spend more time with my mother.

Home was no longer Dunaway Drive. The house my father stopped in front of was different, smaller. The street was not as pretty, but I did not care because I was finally home with my mother and my father, who also seemed happier now that my mother was home.

My mother's speech had improved, so I was able to understand every word she said. The sadness that had overwhelmed her before going to the hospital seemingly disappeared. Now when I looked into her eyes, I could see that they sparkled; her happy spirit had returned. I was happy to have the duty of being her little helper again.

My mother was home, my father had a job, and I finished fourth grade at the David Crockett School in Dallas. Home must have been happy and calm during this time because I have no outstanding memories of this period, only a report card showing that my grades improved in every subject.

I have no memory of my sister being in the house when I returned from St. Joseph's. I was so happy to be back home with my mother, having her all to myself. I selfishly did not seem to miss my sister. I was content knowing that I did not have to share my mother's attention.

My sister did not return to live with us until sometime later. A family picture of my mother, father, sister, and me together in 1967 suggests that my sister returned home when she was five years old after I had completed the fourth grade.

Chapter Two

Family Move to California

Different State, More Tragedy

We moved to California sometime in 1969, confirmed by my father's arrest record for drunk driving in Los Angeles County in November 1969, followed by a petty theft charge in Downey, California, in December 1969. The California school records confirm that I attended seventh grade at the Bell Gardens Junior High School.

Our lives must have calmed down significantly for a year or two because I have no memory of any significant events. My report cards confirm that we continued to live in Dallas through June 1968, where I completed the fifth grade, yet no school records exist for my attendance in the sixth grade.

My memories of living in California begin with the house we moved into on Gotham Street in Bell Gardens. Our house was located at the back of the property lot separated from the front house by a small yard and a driveway. I attended seventh grade at the Bell Gardens Junior High School, which was about a half-mile walk from our house.

Loud music was a staple in our new household. Listening to James Brown, the Temptations, and Stevie Wonder with my parents, dancing to music for my parents, and watching my father guide my mother's partially paralyzed body in dance moves to their favorite songs are the fondest memories I have of the time spent with my parents on Gotham Street.

R&B music transported all of us to a happier place. Watching Mom and Dad dancing, smiling, and laughing gave me hope that everything would be okay. I was joyful and filled with pride when my parents would say to me, "Marie, get up here. Show us your best dance moves." I would happily comply, loving the attention from my parents, who laughed and smiled as I danced without abandon, sometimes accompanied by my mother, who would twirl my sister and me around the floor, giving us tips on how to move our feet and shake our hips to the rhythm of the music. It made me happy to see that my mother still had her joy for dancing. Even though she did not have full use of her right leg or arm, she was still able to sway her hips and laugh easily at my sister and me trying to do the moves she would coach us through.

Music playing in our household usually meant good times for us until my father would start drinking until he passed out or until he became belligerent toward my mother, bringing tension into what was our happy place. Most times, I could sense when my father's drunken behavior was veering from easygoing to unstable—my cue to retreat to my bedroom with my sister to avoid being in close vicinity to him.

My father did not seem to work a lot after we moved to California. He was always home when most of my friends' parents were at work. I would hear some conversations about him going to work to drive trucks. His absence was intermittent for these driving jobs, which meant that he was home a lot more than when we lived in Dallas.

Walking to school is how I met my first friend in the neighborhood, Cindy, who lived in the corner house of our street. Cindy was also in seventh grade, making it easy for me and her to spend a lot of time together. Her house would become a regular place for me to hang out, and I often took my sister with me so she could play with Cindy's younger siblings.

Hanging out at Cindy's home was a fun respite from our household because all of us kids could play in or out of the house, do our homework, and watch television without any concern of a parent being drunk or angry. Cindy's mother, Theresa, always seemed to be in the kitchen cooking something delicious, often inviting my sister and me to stay for dinner if it was okay with our parents.

I tried to stay at Cindy's house as much as possible, so I finally got up the nerve to ask my parents if I could have dinner at Cindy's house. My mother said it was okay, but my father told me he had to meet the parents before allowing me to have dinner with them. I was disappointed and worried, knowing that I had to bring my erratic father to the place where I felt happy and safe. I was concerned that Theresa would not want me at her house once she met my father. I thought that his behavior would be a reflection on me. I could only hope that he would be sober when the introduction took place.

I was embarrassed by my father when I took him to meet Theresa because it seemed like he was drunk, even though I had not seen him drinking during the day. I could tell that Theresa was wary of him as he tried to charm her with compliments. My father, even in an altered state, always had a self-assured presence when he interacted with people. I felt that he was trying too hard to convince Theresa how concerned he was for the safety of his daughters, even though there were complete strangers coming in and out of our house, hanging around to party with my father during the day and sometimes into the nights.

I felt great relief and happiness when my father agreed to allow me to have dinner at Cindy's house whenever I was invited. He actually thanked Theresa for being such a kind neighbor and for keeping an eye on his daughters.

I had just relaxed, happy with this meeting; then my father had to ruin it with his parting words: "Theresa, don't hesitate to call me if either Marie or Faith don't obey your rules. I'll take off my belt and beat their asses if they ever cause you any problems." My father always had to remind us that he was in charge, that he had the power.

Theresa's home was a safe place to be, a good example of what a loving family living happily together looked like. It was nothing like my home. Theresa must have sensed that something was going on in our house because she often told my sister and me that we could come over anytime: "Bring your pajamas to spend the night whenever you want. You are welcome in our house anytime."

Eventually, my parents having people in our house became a daily occurrence. Many times, I would come home from school in the afternoon to see my father and mother in the living room with one, two, or three friends hanging out, drinking, music playing loudly, barely acknowledging that my sister and I were home. The people in our house always seemed to be drunk, sitting in our living room, with heavy smoke hanging in the air, smoke that did not smell like the Pall Mall cigarettes that my parents usually smoked, and sometimes a variety of pills would be spread out on our coffee table, which my father would try to quickly cover with newspapers when I would walk through the living room.

My mother would try to show interest in me by asking me how my day went at school. I would simply reply, "It was okay" because I did not feel like talking about my day, my life, in front of strangers who were trying too hard to be nice to me. I was enjoying the social aspect of school, sometimes putting more effort into making friends and hanging out with friends instead of focusing on schoolwork. I was able to maintain a B average in my first semester of junior high school.

I missed spending time alone with my mother. I missed having her full attention. I felt her drifting away from me and my sister to spend more time hanging with my father and friends. What I did not realize was that my mother was suffering from depression, an illness she would have for the rest of her life.

My bedroom became my retreat until my mother would call my sister and me into the kitchen for dinner or until I asked if I could go to Cindy's house for dinner. When I did stay home for dinner, it was usually only my sister and me with our mother eating at the kitchen table together, while my father would stay with his friends in the living room.

Having dinner with my mother and sister was enjoyable, but at the same time, I felt resentment building within me toward my parents because their friends were clearly more important to them than spending time with my sister and me. After dinner, I would help my mother clear the table and wash the dishes; then she would rejoin the party in the living room while my sister and I were relegated to our bedrooms to do our homework.

We were no longer a family who talked about the day's activities at the dinner table. We no longer watched television together. Our parents no longer took the time to sit with us after dinner or show any interest to help us with homework. Our house on Gotham Street no longer felt like home.

Drugs and Chaos

A few months would pass before it would become apparent to me, what I think Theresa had already known—my father was taking drugs and possibly selling drugs from our home.

My father compiled an extensive arrest record while we were living on Gotham Street. Probation reports confirm that he was arrested for drunk driving, with a twenty-two-day jail sentence dismissed; guilty of the petty theft of prescription drugs, with a $25 fine paid; and found guilty of drug possession when he tossed two plastic bags out of his car window while being pursued by the police for driving in an erratic manner. One bag contained twenty-nine amphetamine tablets, and the other bag had thirty-one grams of marijuana. My father was able to avoid a one-year jail sentence by paying a $250 fine with jail time suspended for four years' probation due to expire in September 1974.

My father's continued heavy drinking would be the catalyst for his drug use, increasing the conflict between him and my mother, usually in the form of physical fights. I would often try to intervene, especially when my father would taunt my mother to hit him, knowing she was no match for him, with her one arm flaying, always inches away from contacting my father as he laughed at her attempts to try to hit or scratch at him, both of them running around the dinner table, playing a sick game of chase.

My father was taunting my mother—"How are you going to hit me when you can't even catch me?"

I wanted to punch my father in the face when I would see him antagonizing my mother. I would plead with my mother to stop trying to hit him—"Mom, stop! Can't you see he is just trying to make you mad? Don't give him the satisfaction of trying to hit him."

I was worried that he would hurt her even more if she actually did catch him. My father's actions toward my mother made me furious; my mother's actions toward my father made me anxious because I knew he could seriously hurt her.

The intensity and frequency of the battles between my parents escalated in the level of violence when my mother, on one occasion, pulled a butcher knife from the kitchen drawer and walked over to my father—who was sitting at the kitchen table in a slouched, drunken, or drug-induced stupor—to stab him in the shoulder and arm a couple of times before he became alert enough to put his forearm up to block the knife. My mother got a few more stabs into his arm before my father was able to knock the knife out of her hand, throwing her to the floor, straddling her, his legs across her body, and slapping her across the face while trying to grab her flailing arm as blood splattered from the wounds on his arm.

My sister and I watched in horror, screaming at my parents to "stop! Please stop! You're going to kill each other!"

My father finally released my mother and rolled over on the floor, lying still for a few minutes, with blood seeping out of his wounds, my mother still screaming obscenities at him, telling him to leave the house.

My father screamed, "If I leave this house, you are fucking going to jail for trying to kill me! Get some towels to help stop this bleeding!"

My sobbing, defeated mother obeyed. They both calmed down, working together to attend to my father's wounds, while I grabbed some wet rags to wipe up blood from the floor. My mother looked so defeated after this incident. I felt so sad for her, thinking how unhappy and frustrated she must have been to think that murdering my father was going to make her life better. Maybe she did not intend to kill him; maybe she just wanted to inflict some pain on him as he so often did to her.

As horrifying as this altercation between my parents was, I remember being thankful that my father had not harmed my mother. He seemed genuinely concerned about her going to jail. Instead, they worked together to patch up his wounds and then assured my sister and me that everything would be okay as they sent us off to bed.

How do you sleep after seeing such a violent act between the two people who are supposed to be taking care of you and your sister? I could not sleep. I lay in my bed, listening, waiting for another outburst between my parents to occur. I was not convinced that their battle was over. Finally, I picked up a book I was reading for English class to replace the scenes I had just witnessed. I read until I fell asleep, with my sister snuggled next to me.

I would never learn what the tipping point was to cause my mother to attack my father with a butcher knife. Maybe she was simply tired of living with his addictions and violent behavior. Sadly, whatever had upset her was not enough to motivate her to leave my father.

We awoke the next morning to get ready for school and went about the day as if nothing tragic had happened the night before. I looked forward to going to school. School was my sanctuary, filled with friends and providing a brief respite from our unstable home life.

Our home was now a place where people came to hang out with my father, mostly men, drinking with my father, listening to music, and using drugs. My father was using drugs and selling drugs. Apparently, my mother had no concern or no choice about the activities taking place in our home because she too would stay up with my father, partying into the night.

My sister was moved to sleep with me in my bedroom to free up her room for some of these partiers to spend the night. There were too many occasions when we would wake up in the morning to get ready for school to see one or two men still in our house, sometimes coming out of our parents' bedroom or still sleeping in what had been my sister's room as we got ready for school.

It made me uncomfortable to see men coming out of my parents' bedroom. In the beginning, it did not make sense to me that they were sleeping with my parents when they could have spent the night on the couch or in my sister's bedroom. At first, I was too naive to understand that my father and mother were having sex with the people they invited into their bedroom. It was from overhearing conversations between my parents that I learned that they were having sex parties. I think these parties provided some income and drugs. I never saw my mother take illegal drugs—she barely drank alcohol—so I maintain the belief that her participation was voluntary, as voluntary as any situation can be for a woman who was battered and abused by her husband.

Some of the activities my father and mother hosted would eventually become apparent and frightening—more people, more drugs. I did my best to keep my sister and myself invisible to avoid the anger of our father and the attention of the strangers in our house who I instinctually felt could cause us harm. I think my fear stemmed from a past incident when one of the men who had been hanging out with my father, drinking and taking drugs in our house, opened the door to the bedroom, where my sister and I were doing homework. This stranger sat on the bed and began asking us questions: "How old are you? Why don't you come out of your room and sit with us?" I pulled my sister close to me so we could huddle together, growing more fearful of having this stranger in our private space, asking us questions.

It seemed like forever before my father appeared and yelled at the man, "Get the fuck away from my girls! Get the fuck out of my house now before I get my gun and kill your ass!"

A positive outcome from this incident was that my sister got her bedroom back and people stopped spending the night at our house.

My anger and resentment toward my parents was wearing on me. They seemingly had little to no concern, depending on my father's state of intoxication, for the safety of their daughters. Our mother was no longer a source of love and affection for my sister and me as she had succumbed to whatever life my father and she had created behind closed doors. They were not keeping us safe in our home.

It was during my junior high school years when I began to feel hopeless and tired of our unsettled home life. The arguments between my parents gradually intensified, with more physical altercations between them, my mother trying to grab at my father's arm, shirt, or hair, anything she could grab to try to hold him still to scream at him, claw at his face, his arms, whatever part of his body was exposed. Mom was no match for my father. He would push her away with such force that she would fall to the floor or stumble, landing violently on furniture that would overturn as her body fell backward.

I would scream, "Stop! Stop fighting! Mom, you are going to get hurt! Stop!"

My parents never seemed to hear my pleas when they were fighting. Eventually, I stopped trying to be the referee of their physical altercations, fearing that I might get hurt; then my sister would have no one to watch out for her safety.

My mother rarely said anything about the fights between her and my father. When she did, it was simply excusing his behavior—"Your daddy sometimes drinks too much, but he loves you and is doing his best to work to take care of us."

I did not agree with my mother's observation, but I was not going to challenge her statement because I had no idea what options we had other than living with our parents.

I learned that it was easier to take my sister to her room or my room, where we would do schoolwork together or watch television until it was time for her to go to bed. Some nights, my father would pass out early, giving us much-needed quiet time, with our mother watching television or reading to my sister.

Looking back, I do not recall my mother talking to us very often about the chaos that was happening in our house, but I know it was affecting her because she started to lash out at my sister and me, grabbing our hair to harshly yank us toward her to yell at us about some chore we forgot to do. Sometimes she would simply grab our hair to shake our heads back and forth in frustration because she thought we were talking back to her. No one was happy in our house.

Nightmare

I was dreaming. I had never felt this warm, pulsating feeling between my legs before. Something was rubbing against my vagina; it felt good. I wanted the dream to continue, but I woke up to the smell of alcohol to see a man fumbling at my panties.

Afraid and confused, I screamed, "Mom! Dad! Mom!"

Suddenly, the man was on top of me, the weight of his body pressing me into the mattress, making it difficult for me to move, his hand pressed down on my mouth, covering my nose so tightly that I could barely breathe. I tried to roll my body over to get out from underneath him.

I pushed at him with my arms, screaming, "Stop! Get off me! Let me go! Mom! Dad! Help me!"

"Shut the fuck up, or I will beat the shit out of you and your mother."

His voice—why does his voice sound familiar to me? The words were also familiar to me. *No, no. This cannot be happening. The voice is my father's voice!*

I kicked my legs harder, bucking my body from side to side, trying to get out from under his weight, hoping that his hand would leave my mouth so I could scream. The more I bucked and bounced, the harder he pressed his hand against my mouth; I could barely catch my breath. I felt like he was going to suffocate me as the palm of his hand tightened around my nose and mouth. I decided to lie very still for a moment, hoping that he would remove his hand from my nose and mouth so I could breathe. I felt his grip loosening.

I was sobbing. "Daddy, it's Marie. Please, please let me go. I can't breathe."

"Are you going to be quiet? I will take my hand away if you stay still and don't make a sound."

I nodded. He slowly took his hand away from my face, whispering, "Don't say a fucking word. Do not call out for your mother. Just lie still. I'm not going to hurt you."

I gasped for several breaths, feeling panicked. I could not stop sobbing. I tried to lie very still, almost holding my breath, hoping that my father would realize that he had made a mistake, hoping he would go away now that he knew I was awake. *Maybe he will realize he is in the wrong bedroom.* I was hoping that in his drunken, drugged-out state, maybe he was thinking that he got into bed with my mother. I tried to gather my thoughts, tried to figure out what was really happening. *Is this really my father holding me down?*

I tried again to push his body with my arms, trying to turn my body sideways to get out from under the weight of him.

"Are you going to lie still, or do you want me to put a pillow over your face? I will fucking kill you and your mother if you call for her again."

I knew his words were true. I had seen him put his hands around my mother's throat. I had seen him drag her across the floor to their bedroom. I had suffered several of his beatings, usually enforced with a belt on my bare legs and buttocks, even my arms when I tried to grab the belt to stop the lashings. I had seen the pleasure he got from antagonizing my mother and watched helplessly as their physical altercations became more violent. I realized that all he cared about was what he always cared about—himself.

In that moment, feeling his force and aggression, I felt that he could and would kill me to get what he wanted. He was not seeing me as his daughter; he was seeing me as an object for him to use as he pleased. I was helpless. I would willingly suffer another beating from him if only I could get away from this nightmare, if only my mother could come and save me.

I lay perfectly still as my father removed his hand from my mouth again, warning me to be quiet—"Do not make a fucking sound."

As he moved down my body, he was fumbling with his pants. I wanted to scream for my mother again. Instead, I placed my pillow over my head and lay as still as I possibly could as tears and snot soaked into my pillowcase. I felt my father's hands aggressively hold me down as he lifted my pajama dress to remove my panties.

I was sobbing, "Stop, stop. God, please make this stop!"

I tried to wriggle free from under him. He threw the pillow to the floor and then reached up to put his forearm on my throat. I could not catch my breath. I was sure he was going to kill me.

"I told you to shut the fuck up. If you lie still and relax, this will feel good."

Slowly, he moved down toward my crotch, slightly releasing the hold on my throat, reminding me to be quiet. He was kissing my vagina.

"See? Doesn't this feel good?"

I did not respond.

"I know it does because you are ready."

I thought, *Ready? Ready for what?*

Suddenly, his entire body was on top of me, and I felt a sharp pain inside my vagina.

I screamed, "Stop! It hurts! It hurts!"

His forearm returned to my throat with more force, force to keep me quiet, enough force to make me feel like I could not breathe. He was forcing himself inside of me, breathing his alcoholic breath into my face. Inside my head, I was repeating, *Mom, Mom, where are you? Help me. Please help me.* However, I was a prisoner under the weight of my father's body. All I could do now was lie as still as possible, trying not to focus on the pain as he plunged into my body over and over, his body weighing so heavily on mine that I felt like I would suffocate. I wished I would suffocate to escape the pain between my legs and the fury in my body. *Please make this nightmare end.*

It seemed like forever before he finally lifted himself off me. I rolled onto my side, sobbing into my sheets, pulling the covers over myself, trying to be invisible, waiting for him to leave my bedroom. I lay still, feeling pain between my legs, trying to cry quietly to avoid his hand on my face again.

My father's parting words to me were "Do not tell your mother about this. Do not tell anyone about this. If you do, you know I will be very angry with you, and you know what can happen if you make me angry."

I was twelve years old.

As I lay on my bed, feeling scared and alone, I felt a cloak of shame surround me as I realized I was enjoying being touched by my father before I knew it was him touching me. I felt more shame because I was too afraid to scream louder. I felt shame because I thought I should have fought harder. *How will I tell my mother? What will she think? What will she do?*

I wanted to wash every inch of my body, but I knew that showering might wake up my sister or cause my father to come back out of my parents' bedroom. Instead, I closed the bathroom door to stand at the sink, lathering a washcloth with soap, my tears falling into the suds. I could barely look at myself in the mirror. The area around my mouth was bright red from my father's hands on my mouth to mute me. My neck was bright red from my father's forearm trying to silence me by taking my breath away. My chest was red from him using his hands and arms to subdue me.

I felt like he had dirtied every part of my body. I scrubbed as hard as I could. I scrubbed the blood off the inside of my thighs and the outside of my vagina. I lathered up the soap bar in my hands to cover my mouth with suds to wash away the sweat from my father's hand. I scrubbed every part of my body that had been touched by my father, stopping several times to press the wet washcloth against my face to muffle my sobs and silent screams.

I returned to my bedroom fearing that my father might come back. I closed my bedroom door, knowing he could still enter because there was no lock on the door. I decided to wedge the back of a small desk chair I had in my bedroom up under the door handle with my laundry basket on top of the chair, knowing these things probably would not keep my father out if he decided to come back but hoping there would be enough noise to make him stop for fear that my sister or mother would hear the noise. I cried myself to sleep, worn out by fear, sadness, and pain, wondering what tomorrow would bring.

I was awake early enough to get to the bathroom and lock the door behind me before my sister woke up. While undressing to take a long, hot shower, I noticed that my panties were stained with blood, the blood reminding me of the pain and fear I had felt while under the weight of my father's body, the blood making me worry that my body had been injured. I began sobbing again, stepping into the shower to turn the water on at full force, turning the hot water faucet up as high as my skin could bear to scrub every inch of my body touched by my father, sobbing into the washcloth. After the shower, I rolled my panties and nightgown up into a knotted ball and then shoved them deep into my backpack to take with me to throw into garbage cans on my way to school.

I was hoping that I could get out of the house before my mother and father woke up. I could not bear the thought of seeing my father or my mother because I knew I would not be able to tell my mother what happened with my father in the house. When would have been the best time for me to tell my mother what had happened to me while she was sleeping? *Would she believe me? What would she say to my father? Would she kick my father out of the house? Would my father admit that he had raped me? Why did he rape me?*

When I opened my bedroom door, the smell of coffee hit my nostrils. *Oh no. Who is awake?* The thought of seeing my father sickened me; the thought of seeing my father before I could talk to my mother frightened me. I froze, contemplating what to do. I convinced myself that my father would not be up this early because he had been drunk last night. I slowly walked down the hallway into the kitchen to see my mother sitting at the kitchen table, drinking her morning cup of coffee like every other morning.

"Morning, Marie. Why are you up and ready for school so early?"

My mother's question made me realize she did not hear what had happened to me during the night. I was too afraid to tell my mother that my father had raped me. I was too ashamed to tell her that I was not able to make him stop. I was afraid that my mother would not love me anymore if I told her what my father had done to me.

At the same time, I felt resentment building inside me because my mother had no idea what had happened to me during the night. *How could she not hear anything?* We lived in a small house. I felt that she should *know* what had happened to her daughter. *She should know! I should not have to say out loud that my father raped me. She should be able to see that there is something different about me.* My body was filled with so much anger, making me feel trapped in this house, which no longer felt safe to me. I had to get out.

I abruptly told Mother, "I am leaving early to meet a couple of friends at school to talk about a book we have to report on during class today."

Looking back, I think I was worried that she would not believe me; I could not bear the thought of my mother not believing me. I was also worried about violent repercussions from my father. I did not want my mother or myself harmed because of what had happened to me. It was over. I just wanted to forget it had ever happened.

Forgetting would not be possible as my father would continue his nighttime intrusions into my bedroom, always when he was drunk or high. He was forcing himself on top or me or making me masturbate him, which was almost as painful as being raped because the physical closeness to my father disgusted me. Waiting for him to ejaculate was much too intimate to bear. I kept my head turned away to avoid looking at him or any part of his body, imagining that if I tugged hard enough, I might be able to rip his penis off or, at the very least, make it hurt so he would not want me to continue. Instead, he would grab my hand, telling me to stop being so rough, putting his hand over mine to show me how tight to squeeze and how fast to move. Feeling his hand on mine made me sob, which made him angry.

"STOP crying. This will be over quicker if you stop crying and do what I tell you."

I could not stop crying because I was so filled with anger that he was forcing me do this. I hated my father with every cell of my body. I wanted him to stop coming into my bedroom.

I was close to convincing myself to stop, even if it meant a beating, when he jerked my hand away from his penis and then pushed me down on the bed, commanding me to take off my pajamas and touch myself.

I said, "I don't know what you mean."

He growled, "You are fucking stupid. Touch yourself like this." He rubbed my breasts roughly with one hand and then started to move his other hand down my legs, toward my vagina.

I did not want him to touch me anymore, so I pushed his hand away and quickly said, "I get it, I get it."

I took off my top and closed my eyes so I would not have to look at his face as I massaged my breasts, trying to hum quietly to block out his disgusting grunts.

Falling asleep became difficult for me. I was always on alert, not knowing when the next assault was coming. I would often persuade my sister to sleep with me because I knew my father would not come into my room if she were with me. Sometimes I would stay in her room to read her a story so I could fall asleep next to her.

One evening, during dinner, my father asked my sister why she had been sleeping in my bedroom.

My sister said, "Because Marie wants me to sleep with her. She said I keep her bad dreams away."

I swear my father looked at me with a smirk on his face before he said, "Well, Marie is old enough to take care of herself. I do not think she needs her seven-year-old sister in her bed to keep the boogeyman away."

Just like that, my security blanket was taken away from me.

I began having hostile feelings toward my mother because I felt that she had to know that something was happening to me. I lashed out at her, not doing what she told me to do, hoping that she would sense that something was seriously wrong with me. I needed my mother to rescue me, yet I was not brave enough to ask for her help. I was also fearful that my father would hurt the both of us if my mother confronted him.

One day, while showering, I panicked when blood began to run down my legs. My first thought was that there was something wrong with my body because of my father's sexual attacks, but the blood flow was different this time; there was a lot of blood. I yelled for my mother to come into the bathroom. Through tears, I told her that I was bleeding.

"Marie, calm down. Calm down. It's only your period. You've started your period."

"How do you know?" I cried. "How do you know all of this blood isn't coming from my injured vagina?"

My mother looked at me with confusion on her face. "Marie, what are you talking about? You don't get injured from your period."

"I'm not injured from my period. I'm injured from being raped by your husband! He comes into my bedroom at nights when you are asleep to rape me and do other things!"

Instantly, I felt great relief from telling my mother that I was being raped. Then I immediately regretted blurting out this information when I saw the confusion on her face change to disbelief.

"Marie, what are you talking about? Your father sleeps in bed with me every night."

"How do you know what he is doing? You're asleep!"

I told her that he had been coming into my bedroom for months to have sex with me. I told her how he had threatened to hurt me and her if I told anyone. I told her how the first time he had raped me, he threatened to kill me and her if I told anyone. I told her how he had almost smothered me with a pillow, how he had made me gasp for air by holding his arm on my throat. I told her how afraid I had been to say anything because I believed he would hurt us.

"Marie, I will have to talk to your father about this."

"Talk to him! Why would you talk to him about it? Do you think he is going to tell the truth? You need to make him stop. You need to pay attention to when he is not in bed with you. Now that I have told you, I will scream as loud as I can, fight as hard as I can when he comes into my room so you can hear me and make him stop!"

The look on mother's face made me feel like she did not believe a word I was saying to her. She just looked at me, stunned. I knew she was going to tell my father what I had told her, but I did not care because I was feeling a sense of relief from telling her the truth, telling her that my father was sexually assaulting me. I knew there would be repercussions after my mother spoke with my father about my confession. I waited in fear for whatever was going to happen next.

That evening, after my sister was in bed asleep, my parents asked me to sit down with them in the living room to talk. I was afraid of what was about to happen. My father was eerily calm, asking me to sit down on the couch between him and my mother. I obeyed, my mother looking at me indifferently.

My father said, "Marie, your mother tells me you think I did something to you while you were asleep in your bed."

I began to cry. "I don't *think* you did something to me. I *know* you raped me!"

"Marie, I would never want to hurt you, especially in that way."

I looked at my father with tears streaming down my face. "But you did hurt me, not once, not twice. You know you raped me many times."

"Marie, if I were in your room harming you, wouldn't you scream for your mother?"

"I wanted to scream, but you said you would kill me and Mom. Plus, you would smother me when I did try to scream." I looked at my mother. "Mom, why don't you believe me? Why are you taking his side?"

She replied, "Marie, I'm not taking sides. I am trying to understand what happened to you. Your father and I think something traumatic may have happened to you that you cannot or do not want to tell us."

"I'm telling you what happened to me. I'm telling you now that he raped me."

My father tried to move closer to me.

I backed away toward my mother, crying, "Mom, please believe me. Why don't you believe me?"

My mother simply looked at me and then looked at my father as if she was unable to see clearly without his input.

My father said, "Marie, I'm sorry if, in one of my drunken episodes, I may have stumbled into your bedroom and fallen on your bed or touched you, thinking you were your mother, but that can be the only thing that happened, or you would have screamed." He looked at my mother. "Did you ever hear Marie screaming?"

My mother shook her head. I was stunned that my mother was unable to consider that what I was telling her was the truth. I realized that my father, the narcissistic king of deflection who never took responsibility for his bad behaviors and poor decisions, was convincing my mother of his innocence. I realized that she was going to accept his explanation instead of the truth. It was probably easier for my mother to believe that my father did not rape me than to believe that he would do such a terrible thing to his daughter—or was she too afraid of him to challenge his explanation?

I felt abandoned and furious. I stood up and started screaming at my mother, "I do not believe you are taking his word over mine! Why would

I lie?" I turned to my father and screamed, "I WAS RAPED BY YOU! I HATE YOU! I WISH YOU WERE NOT MY FATHER!"

I ran to my bedroom, slamming the door as violently as I possibly could, throwing myself on my bed, sobbing myself to sleep.

The sexual assaults by my father stopped.

My efforts to regain control of my body and self-worth began.

Trouble, Truancies, and Neighbors

Before I was raped by my father, I had been a fairly happy twelve-year-old, attending seventh grade at the Bell Gardens Junior High School. I was maintaining B average grades. I had lots of friends, and I felt happy and normal when I was out of our house, away from my parents' disruptive behaviors.

It was always easy for me to make friends at school, giving me options to hang out at their houses or at school, doing homework to avoid having to go home until absolutely necessary. School and friends were my lifeline to normalcy. In school, I was like everyone else—taking classes, doing schoolwork, hanging with friends.

After the sexual assaults, my grades and attitude changed for the worse. By the beginning of seventh grade, second quarter, my class photo showed a young girl with sad, tired eyes and a half smile, trying her best to be normal, even though she was feeling lost and lonely in her own home.

I was sad, believing that my mother no longer cared about me. I felt abandoned by her because she had believed my father instead of believing me. She never once took the time to sit down with me to discuss the rape accusation I had made against my father; nor had she tried to offer me any words of comfort. I believed that my mother no longer loved me. I felt that I was somehow less than her daughter Marie because I had been raped by my father. I believed that my mother thought less of me because I had been raped by my father, or worse, she really did not believe me. I could not understand why she would choose to believe my father instead of me.

When my father was not around, I would not obey my mother because I was so angry at her for not standing up for me against my father. I would not do anything she would ask me to do without argument, sometimes ignoring her completely by not doing the chores she would tell me to do. I was so mean to my mother, often causing her to call me a "little bitch," which hurt me but, at the same time, made me feel vindicated because I felt like I was punishing my mother for not believing me.

My bad behavior toward my mother prompted my father to frequently wield the belt on me, telling me to stop disrespecting my mother as he delivered the lashings. I felt like I had gained some control back by not doing what I was told. Even though the whippings hurt, I continued to disobey both of them.

My father, returning home from a night of drinking, would pull me out of bed to wash the dinner dishes if I had been so bold to ignore my mother's request to clean up after dinner.

He would push me into the kitchen as I cried, "I'm sorry. I will do the dishes in the morning before school. I need to sleep."

My father would reply, "You should have thought of needing sleep before you went to bed without doing what your mother told you."

He would sit at the dining room table, watching me wash dishes, usually lecturing me on why I should not disrespect my mother. I wanted to tell my father that I had learned how to disrespect my mother from him because he was always disrespecting her. Instead, I chose to avoid antagonizing him so I could go back to bed.

I spent most of the final semester of seventh grade finding ways to disobey my father's rules. I would ditch school with friends, stealing clothes from department stores, stealing mail from mailboxes, opening envelopes, looking for cash. We even stole a car that had keys in the ignition. Of course, none of us knew how to drive, so after several minutes of zigzagging down the residential street, we realized that we might crash and get hurt, so we turned off the car engine and ran away, leaving the car in the middle of the street with the keys still in the ignition.

Our crime spree came to an end when we decided to revisit the White Front department store we had successfully shoplifted from before. Our plan was to take the department store shopping bags from behind an unattended checkout booth and then fill the bags with as many clothing items as possible. Then we would return to the checkout booth to tear the receipt paper off the cash register to staple to our bags and then walk out the store with the bags.

Unfortunately, we had stolen from this White Front store location so many times before that the security guard recognized us and kept a close eye on us as soon as we entered the store. He must have called the police as soon as he saw us putting stolen items into the shopping bag because the police were waiting for us on the sidewalk as soon as we exited the store.

The police officers asked us to explain what we were doing with a bag full of merchandise that we had not paid for. We simply told them we wanted new clothes. We were escorted by the two officers to the back seat of the police car, where they told us to stay while they talked to the store security guard. One officer stood by the car door closest to us, while the other officer took the report. We did not say much to each other while we were sitting in the back seat of the police car. We knew we were in serious trouble. When the officers finished taking the incident report, they opened the car door to tell us that they were going to take us to the police station, where they would call our parents to come pick us up. I was more afraid of the punishment I was going to receive from my father than I was of going to jail.

We got to sit together outside the office of the police officer while he made calls to our parents. My friend, knowing how afraid I was of my father, tried her best to console me by trying to convince me that my parents probably would not answer the phone; then her parents could take me home—no such luck for me. The police officer let us know that my friend's parents were on the way to pick her up and that my father was on his way to pick me up. After my friend left with her parents, I was alone with my thoughts, anguishing over what my punishment would be. I was not looking forward to going home with my father.

As soon as my father walked into the office, he was greeted by the police officer. I watched as my father shook the hand of the officer, offering apologies for having to waste his valuable time dealing with teenage girls who thought they were smart and knew everything about everything.

"What's a parent to do when their child thinks she knows everything already? Kids these days."

Watching my father behave in a friendly, pleasant way with the police officer made me anxious because I had witnessed his condescending tone so many times. I knew he was actually seething inside.

I was released to my father, who put his hand firmly around my left arm to guide me to the car. I barely closed the car door before his tirade started.

"YOU ARE SO FUCKING STUPID! HOW LONG HAVE YOU BEEN SKIPPING SCHOOL?"

"I have no idea. Maybe if you looked at my report cards like Mom does, you would know."

Backhand slap to the face. I refused to give him the satisfaction of seeing me cry. I gulped back tears. Though it was painful, I felt some satisfaction knowing I had pissed my father off big time because he had to pick me up at the police station. It felt good to disappoint him.

"DO NOT FUCKING TALK TO ME WITH THAT TONE. I'M THE ADULT HERE. YOU ARE A FUCKING CHILD WHO IS SO STUPID, SHE THINKS SHE CAN STEAL SHIT FROM A STORE AND WALK OUT OF THAT STORE WITHOUT BEING NOTICED."

"My friend and I have done it before."

He grabbed my chin roughly, pulling my face close to his, forcing me to look directly into his eyes as he spat out, "I GUARANTEE YOU WILL NOT BE SHOPLIFTING OR SKIPPING SCHOOL AGAIN. NOW KEEP YOUR FUCKING MOUTH SHUT. We will talk more about this when we get home."

Sitting in the car close to my father was very uncomfortable for me. I did not like being close to him. Being close to him filled my entire body with fear. Being close to him in a confined space reminded me of when his body was on top of me. Being close to him made me want to jump out of the car. Instead, I remained quiet and still, staring out the windshield. Sitting in such close proximity to my father made me feel like prey as I wondered what physical punishment he would impose upon me once we got home.

My father's tirade continued when we stepped into our house. He yelled at my mother for not telling him I had many absences from school.

"WHAT THE FUCK WERE YOU THINKING SIGNING HER REPORT CARD THAT HAD NGA?" (This stood for "No grade possible until excessive absence stops." A parent conference needed to be scheduled.)

My mother meekly replied, "Marie is still passing her classes. I did not think I needed to mention her absences to you since she is doing okay in her classes."

"I'M FUCKING SURROUNDED BY IDIOTS. A MOTHER WHO LETS HER DAUGHTER DO WHATEVER THE FUCK SHE WANTS. A DAUGHTER WHO THINKS SHE IS THE SMARTEST FUCKING PERSON IN THIS HOUSE."

Watching my father berate my mother—who had become a shell of her once vibrant, happy self—made me angry and sad. I was unable to keep my mouth shut. "IF MOM AND I ARE FUCKING IDIOTS, IT'S BECAUSE WE LIVE WITH YOU, BECAUSE YOU ARE SO FUCKING STUPID, YOU CANNOT EVEN TAKE CARE OF YOUR FAMILY! ALL YOU CAN DO IS GET DRUNK, TAKE DRUGS, AND HURT US."

"What did you just say to me?"

"You heard me. We would be better off without you in our lives."

My mother cried, "Marie, stop!"

"I WILL NOT STOP. I AM SICK OF SEEING HIM HURT YOU, SICK OF YOU LETTING HIM HURT YOU AND ME."

My father yelled, "YOU ARE GODDAMN RIGHT I AM GOING TO HURT YOU IF YOU KEEP TALKING TO YOUR MOTHER AND ME IN THAT TONE!"

"GO AHEAD! HURT ME! YOU CANNOT POSSIBLY HURT ME ANY MORE THAN YOU ALREADY HAVE!"

My father, red-faced and furious, began to take off the belt from around his waist, my mother pleading with me to tell him I was sorry for what I had said, but I was not sorry for what I had said. I was sorry that I had not said these words sooner.

My father grabbed my arm, trying to pull me to the couch, but I fought as hard as I could. I scratched at him, kicked at him, ran from him, screamed at him to leave me alone. I felt like I was fighting for my life. At one point, my mother attempted to pull at my father's shirt and arm, yelling at him to calm down, but he pushed her so hard, she fell to the ground, landing hard. My father momentarily stopped to look at my mother, giving me the opportunity to push away from him, to run to my mother to see if she was okay. My mother was in tears but said she was okay.

Suddenly, my father's focus returned to me. He grabbed my arm, overpowering me, pulling at my dress. I felt like he was trying to tear it off my body to get to my panties, to pull them off to expose my bare bottom and thighs.

I yelled at him, "YOU WILL NOT TAKE MY PANTIES OFF! YOU CAN WHIP ME WITH MY PANTIES ON. YOU WILL HAVE TO KILL ME BEFORE I EVER LET YOU TAKE MY PANTIES OFF AGAIN."

My father would deliver the worst beating upon me today, with hard slaps across my face, causing me to feel disoriented until I felt him grab me by my hair to hold me down for the most painful belt lashings to my legs and butt—so many lashes, so much bleeding, it would take weeks for the wounds to completely heal so I could wear dresses again. My mother had to write me a note to be excused from PE class because I did not want to be embarrassed by my welts.

Fighting my father that day helped me regain my self-worth. I fought back. I finally fought back. I was unable to fight back when he had raped me, but today I fought back with all my might. Today I realized I was strong. I may not have won the physical battle, but I won the mental battle of regaining my self-respect. I knew that if I could survive my father, I could do anything.

I was lonely when I was not in school. I knew I was safe at school with my friends, but I did not want to bring any of my friends to my house because I never knew what state of mind my father would be in or if there would be strangers over, partying with him. If my father were not at home, I could hang out with my mother and sister, watching television or doing homework. If my father were home, I would stay in my bedroom.

Shame made me distance myself from my friend Cindy and her family. I stopped going to Cindy's house on a regular basis after her mother asked me if everything was okay.

"You look tired and unhappy. How are things going at home?"

I was too ashamed to tell Theresa about my father's sexual assault. I was uncertain of the repercussions my confession would bring upon my mother and me. More importantly, I was afraid that Theresa would see me differently. I could not shake my fear and shame.

I wish I had told Theresa the truth on that day when she asked me if everything was okay. I now know she would have helped me because she would know that being raped was not my fault. She would know how to safely get me out of my parents' house, but I was too afraid of the unknown. Would my father be put in jail? If my father did go to jail, how would my mother be able to take care of my sister and me? Would my mother even want me to live with her?

Looking back, none of these scenarios should have been my burden to bear, but no one was telling children in 1970 where they could go to seek help when their parents were the people causing them harm. I made a promise to myself to focus on graduating high school so I could get a good job and move away from my parents as quickly as possible.

Home was the last place I wanted to be when my father was around, so I replaced my safe haven at Cindy's house with hanging out with the neighbors, a girl who I thought was a few years older than me who lived with her father. She was always friendly and always seemed to be home, not attending school or working. I just assumed that she had already graduated from high school. She would encourage me to come over anytime, which I did often to get out of my house and to spite my father, who had argued with her father for reasons unknown to me. My father's dislike for our neighbors increased my motivation to hang out at their house as often as possible.

I shared some of what was going on in my house—my parents fighting, my father drinking or doing drugs. My new friend listened intently, telling me she could understand why I would not want to be home with so much going on. She told me I could come over anytime to do homework or just hang out.

My neighbor was like a big sister to me, making sure I finished my schoolwork before we would hang out, watching television or listening to music. I was very comfortable with her. We would hang out often in her living room, watching television together or me doing my homework, sitting next to her on the couch while she listened to music.

One day we started wrestling and tickling each other to see who could make the other laugh hard enough until snot came out of our noses. She eventually got the upper hand, straddling me, tickling me until I begged for relief from a side ache.

She said, "I'll stop tickling you if you let me kiss you."

"Kiss me? Okay, but you cannot tickle me again after you are done giving me a kiss."

"Okay," she said, and then she leaned down to kiss me on the mouth.

It was not a peck-on-the-lips kiss like I was expecting. It was a full wet kiss with tongue. I did not stop her. I liked the kiss. She sat up, still straddling my body, and asked me if I liked the kiss. I said no, I did not like having her spit in my mouth. We laughed and started wrestling again. Truthfully, I liked being kissed. I liked her tenderness. I liked the feel of her soft lips on mine and the warm sensation I felt between my legs when we kissed.

It was easy to hang out at the neighbors' house more than stay at home since my parents were preoccupied with partying at our house again with friends whom my father would invite over. My parents did not seem to care about how much time I spent next door with the neighbors, and I was happy being away from home because I did not have to be around my father.

I noticed that my friend and her father had a very close relationship, somehow different from how I had seen Cindy interact with her parents. They were more like friends than daughter and father, often joking, tickling each other, having fun together like I had never seen watching other parents with their kids. I thought that maybe older kids acted more like friends with their parents.

One day, when I was over doing homework at their kitchen table, my friend called out to me to come to her bedroom. She wanted to show me something. When I got to her bedroom, she was not there.

"Where are you?" I called out.

"Keep coming down the hallway to the other bedroom."

When I stepped into the bedroom doorway, I saw her lying in bed on top of the cover next to her father.

"What are you two doing?" I asked.

My friend asked me to come sit down on the bed with her. I told her I was good standing.

"There is something I have to tell you. I am not his daughter. I am his girlfriend."

At first, I did not know what to say. I just stood in the doorway, looking at the two of them calmly, lounging in bed like everything was normal. I was processing what I had just heard. My feelings were hurt because she had been lying to me for months. "Why have you been lying to me?"

I did not wait for an answer. I ran down the hallway, away from them because I did not want them to see me crying. I quickly gathered up my things so I could leave their house.

She ran after me. "Joannes, sit down, honey. Let me explain." She told me that they could not tell me the truth sooner because of the argument they had had with my father about drugs. "Your father tried to sell drugs to us a couple of times. We finally got pissed off and told your father to stop coming around our house trying to sell drugs. We do not use drugs."

They thought that my father would not allow me to come over if he knew they were a couple.

"We decided to tell you the truth about our relationship because we care about you, and I know I can trust you to keep our secret."

I said, "You look too young to be his girlfriend. He looks like he is my father's age. How can he be your boyfriend? How old are you?"

She replied, "I am nineteen years old."

I thought, *Gross! Why would a teenager want to be with a man that looked old enough to be her father?* I kept the thoughts to myself and simply looked at her. She continued to explain how people could be judgmental when they see a young lady with a much older man, so they did not make it a point to tell people they were a couple.

I felt indifferent after they had answered all of my questions. She was my friend who happened to like older guys. She and I walked back to the bedroom, where her boyfriend was still sitting in bed, watching television. He asked us if everything was cool. We said yes. Then I asked them to tell the story of how they had met. I listened while still trying to process that they were girlfriend and boyfriend. Whatever their story, it did not take away from the feelings I had for her. The three of us just hung out the rest of the day, watching shows until it was time for me to go home.

We returned to our routine of hanging out together at their house. My friend would watch television in the bedroom while I did my homework; then we would hang out together.

One day, while we were lying on the bed together, watching TV, she leaned over to whisper in my ear, "I noticed how much you liked it when I kissed you before. Do you want me to kiss you again?"

I looked at her and nodded, lying still as she kissed my face and then moved to kiss my lips. I leaned in to kiss her back.

She said, "Close your eyes and relax. I am going to make you feel good today."

I closed my eyes to concentrate on how good it felt to be touched gently. She slowly moved down my body, kissing my chest.

Suddenly, I felt more weight on the bed. I opened my eyes to see her boyfriend approaching her from behind. My body jolted up. I felt a sickening panic come over me. Why was he reaching to touch me? He was old enough to be my father. In that moment, he became my father.

I jumped out of bed and said I was leaving. My friend tried to encourage me to stay.

"Don't you want to play with us?"

"I never said I wanted to play with both of you! I just want to go home."

Tears fell from my eyes as I got up to run down the hallway, only stopping to grab my things off their kitchen table and then running to the back of my house, where I tried to stay out of sight from my parents until I could stop crying.

I never went back inside our neighbors' house. My mother often asked me why I stopped hanging out with my friend. I told her I got bored; plus, she had to do some work for her father.

A few months passed since I had run away from their house when I heard my father tell my mother that they had moved out—"Supposedly, he got a job in another state." I was happy to hear this news because I was stressed whenever I had to pass by their house. I am not sure what caused the stress; maybe I worried that I could be persuaded to hang out with them again. I did miss our friendship, but I was too hurt, angry, and somewhat scared to trust her again.

Looking back, I wonder if I was being groomed to eventually participate in sexual activities with them. I wondered if she was really nineteen years old. I wondered if their relationship was voluntary for her.

My First Angels

Even though I had lived in a Catholic home for girls for six months when I was nine years old, I would eventually lose my belief that God or any higher power existed because I could not comprehend how God would allow any child to suffer physical and mental pain. Maturity, along with my recognition of the value of higher powers that exist beyond organized religion, made me reevaluate how I had been telling my story. I came to realize that as traumatic as my childhood story was, it would have been worse if I had ignored the guides and opportunities that manifested to help me at critical points in my life.

The first guide to appear in my life at a crucial point was a man whom my father and mother allowed to live with us for a brief period on Gotham Street. I will call him Guide One to protect his identity. He was just another stranger my father brought into our home from (I always assumed) a bar. I like to think that my mother had some say as to whether or not these people stayed at our house. I never heard her protest or refuse to participate in the drinking or drug parties that my father often hosted. Looking back, I wonder how much of a choice she had in any of the activities that were seemingly arranged by my father since he was always the one bringing people into our house. I never saw my mother with friends of her own.

This male friend of my parents often hung out at our house, drinking with my father. I would see him walk out of my parents' bedroom in the morning. I would see him sitting on our living room couch, watching television. Seeing him in our house all the time started to annoy me because I did not know why he was in our house all the time. My father and mother never explained anything to me and my sister; they just did what they wanted to do while Faith and I went about trying to be invisible in our own home. It seemed strange to me that this man slept in my parents' bedroom, but I did not want to think too much about the possibilities that would involve him, my mother, and my father.

He lived with us for a few weeks before I thought I should get to know him better since it appeared that he was not leaving our house anytime soon, so I sat next to him on the couch one night and asked him to help me with homework. I did not need help with my homework; I just thought it was an easy way to interact with him so I could figure out why he was living with us.

Sometimes being young and unaware of the consequences allows you the freedom to venture toward things that might make you hesitate when you are older. This stranger would eventually become someone I came to trust. Instinctually, I knew he would not harm me even though the circumstances would suggest that I should not have trusted him.

He would be in our house when I got home from school. He would sometimes eat dinner with us, and he was sometimes around when my father decided to slap me or hit me with his belt because he thought I was disrespecting him or not doing what I was told.

He would often say to my father, "Hey, man. Why are you always hitting your kid? She's just being a kid."

My father would reply, "She *is* a kid—a kid who needs to learn she is not in charge."

I did not care about being in charge. I just wanted to be left alone, to exist in our home peacefully, but my feelings of disdain for the way my father treated my mother and me would simmer inside me until his quest for control would anger me and I would push back. Anger was the only emotion I could feel for my father since the sexual assault.

Our most frequent battles would occur when my father would come home drunk, usually after 8:00 p.m., to see dirty dishes in the sink from the dinner my mother, sister, and I had together.

He would burst into my bedroom, yelling, "Marie, why the fuck haven't you washed the dishes yet?"

"Because I told Mom I would do them after I finished my homework."

"You do not TELL your mother anything. You do what she TELLS you."

"You know what I mean. Mom said I could do my homework first."

"No, I don't know what the fuck you mean. Get your goddamn ass into the kitchen and wash the dishes!"

"Can't I just finish my reading assignment?"

His answer was always no, followed by "Shut your smartass mouth and get in the kitchen now to do the fucking dishes."

I made the mistake of yelling back at him, "You're not doing anything! Why don't YOU do the dishes if it so important to you that they get done right this minute?"

He just looked at me and began to undo his belt from his pants loops. He seethed, "Do not use that fucking tone of voice with me. You better get into the kitchen now to wash the goddamn dishes!"

"Can't the dishes wait until I am done reading?"

No verbal reply came from my father, just the preparation of him unbuckling his belt for another beating.

"Okay, I will do the stupid dishes."

I jumped off my bed, hoping to run past him to the kitchen, but he stood in between me and the door.

He grabbed my arm and said, "You are goddamn right you will wash the stupid dishes." He grabbed me by the hair and started to pull me toward the kitchen.

I was yelling, "You're hurting me! Let go of my hair! I said I would do the dishes!"

I tried to hold onto my father's arm to lessen the hold he had on my hair, but he yanked my arm off his, pulling my hair even more, which made me cry. I could only try to keep up with his pace into the kitchen for relief from the hair pulling.

Guide One appeared behind my father, putting both of his hands firmly on my father's shoulders. "Hey, man. Why don't let go of Marie's hair so she can go do the dishes that you asked her to do?"

My father released my hair from his grip, turned to Guide One, and said, "Take your fucking hands off me and mind your own fucking business."

"Hey, man. I'm just trying to be helpful. It's late. You're tired. Your kids are tired. Just let Marie do what you asked her to do so we can all relax and get a good night's rest."

I managed to squeeze by my father and Guide One into the kitchen, where I frantically started to do the dishes, hoping my father would not come after me.

Guide One came in several minutes later to tell me he had managed to calm my father down and gotten him to sit on the couch in the living room with my mother to watch television. "Don't worry about your father anymore tonight. Just finish the dishes and go back into your bedroom."

Through tears of relief, I said, "Thank you. I'm glad you're here."

Lesson learned. Fifty years later, I still cannot go to bed with dirty dishes in the kitchen sink unless I am sick.

Guide One's act of kindness made me feel safer in our house when he was around. Instead of resenting him for living in our house, I now appreciated that he was around to handle my irrational, angry father. I wanted to get to know him, to spend more time with him. It was nice to have a friend around who knew how to calm down my father. I could tell that my mother was also comfortable around him, lighting up during conversations with him. Seeing my mother at ease with him gave me the assurance that he was a nice guy, making me feel more comfortable around him, looking up to him as a protector while also developing strong feelings of affection for him.

I missed being loved. I missed feeling safe. I did not feel loved by my parents. I had not felt loved since my friend had moved away. I'm sure I was at the height of puberty, thinking that sexual feelings were love. I was grasping for anyone who was kind, who made me feel safe and loved.

My behavior toward Guide One became inappropriate. Sometimes, when my parents were not in the house, I would sit on the couch next to him to watch television. I would kiss his cheek or his neck, laying my head on his shoulder.

"What are you doing, girl?" he said, chuckling. "You better sit still and watch television before you get us both in trouble."

I coyly said, "I want you to know I love you."

He chuckled again. "You're going to love a lot of boys between now and when you get married. I'm too old for you."

"How old are you?" I asked.

"Twice your age."

His age had no impression on me. I knew he was kind. He was cute. Most importantly, he knew how to handle my father and protect me. He was the first person I saw my father actually listen to. He was someone my father appeared to respect. Respecting others was not a trait that my father typically exhibited toward others.

One night my parents went grocery shopping, taking my little sister with them, leaving me alone in the house with Guide One so I could do my homework. He was sitting on the living room couch, watching television, when I decided to sit close to him to do my homework. I could not concentrate sitting that close to him. I wanted to kiss him.

Several minutes passed before I impulsively put my books aside to straddle his lap. Facing him, I pressed my lips against his. He kissed me back, pressing his tongue between my lips. I got that warm, wonderful feeling between my legs again as he pressed against me. I thought, *He does like me.*

He started to move his hands over my fully clothed body. His strong hands were massaging my chest. Then he suddenly pulled away to whisper in my ear, "I'm sorry, Marie. This isn't right."

"Why are you sorry? I feel good. Do you feel good?"

"Yes, of course, I feel good. I really do care about you, but this is wrong. You are only thirteen years old. I could get in a lot of trouble for being with you like this."

"You will not get in trouble if we do not tell anyone. I will not tell anyone. Only you and I will know."

"Yes, only you and I will know what just happened. It will be our secret. But you have to understand that you and I will not do this again."

I started to cry because I felt like I had done something wrong to make him tell me that we would not be able to be close again. He explained that he could go to jail for what had just happened because I was a minor and he was an adult. He reassured me that he would continue to care about me and would be around for a while longer to make sure I, my mother, and my sister were going to be okay.

Guide One made sure we were never alone together again, which made me sad, but I was happy he was still around to be my friend. His time at our house lessened after he got a full-time job. Then he was spending most of his free time hanging out with Theresa, Cindy's mother. I am not sure when or how he and Theresa became friends. They may have been more than friends since he was spending nights at Theresa's instead of at our house. Initially, I was a little jealous that he and Theresa liked each other, but I got over it because they were my favorite adults. Guide One hanging out at Cindy's house gave me another reason to spend as much time as I could with my friend Cindy.

He would still come over to hang out with my father and mother, checking in on me and my sister. I think he may have worked with my father, or they were in the same trucking business because the two of them seemed to talk about work a lot.

During one of his visits, my father and mother got into an argument that moved from our living room to their bedroom. Eventually, my parents screaming at each other was followed by thudding sounds, followed by my mother screaming, "Stop! Stop hitting me!"

Guide One told me to go to my sister's room to make sure she was still asleep and to stay in the room with her until he came to get us. My sister was still asleep. I just stood by her closed bedroom door, trying not to cry as I heard more of my mother's screams, followed by loud noises that sounded like something or someone was being thrown against a wall.

Finally, the noises stopped. I thought I heard the door to the backyard slam, but I was too afraid to look out to see who was still in the house.

Several minutes passed before I heard my mother's voice crying, "Marie? Marie, where are you?"

I opened the bedroom door to see my mother standing before me with a black eye, blood running from her nose and her hair sticking up in all directions like someone had tried to pull her hair out. My father often pushed my mother or twisted her good arm behind her back to force her to do what he wanted, but this was the first time I had seen her bruised and bloody.

I started to cry. "Mom, are you all right? Do you need to go to the hospital?"

"I will be okay, Marie. Come help me wash up and change my clothes."

"Where is Guide One? Did he have to fight Daddy to stop him from hurting you?"

"He calmed your father down enough to get him out of the house, hopefully for the night."

I screamed at her, "Mom, why do you stay with Daddy when he keeps hurting us?"

Instead of answering my question, my mother simply said, "Help me get cleaned up so we can get to bed."

I experienced my first feeling of resentment toward my mother when she did not respond to my question. I felt like she did not care about our safety. I was too young and ignorant to understand that my mother was a battered woman who suffered from depression and low self-esteem, which prevented her from seeking help.

A couple of days later, when I was hanging out with Cindy at her house, Guide One and Theresa asked me to come sit in the living room with them. They wanted to talk to me.

Guide One began. "Marie, what is going on in your house is not right. Your father should not be beating on your mother. He certainly should not be beating you. He seems to be getting more explosive, and I am worried about the safety of you and your sister."

Theresa said, "Honey, I'm sorry I did not realize how bad your living circumstances at home had become. Has your father done other things to hurt you or your sister?"

I wanted to tell Theresa that my father had come into my bedroom when my mother was asleep to rape me, but I was too embarrassed to tell her with Guide One sitting close by. I replied, "Yes, he has done more than just hitting or whipping me. Can I talk to you about it another time when it's just you and me?"

Guide One immediately said, "I will step outside so you can talk to Theresa about this now."

Sobbing, I told Theresa that my father had come into my room several times to have sex with me. I told her that I wanted to tell her sooner, but I was too embarrassed and could not stand the thought of her not believing me. I told her that when I got my period, I told my mother that my father had raped me and she did not believe me; she told my father what I had said. Of course, he denied doing anything to me, and my mother believed him and not me. I thought that if my mother did not believe me, why would anyone else believe me?

Theresa put her arms around me and said, "I am so sorry, honey, that you have been going through this. I am sorry that you felt you could not tell me. None of this is your fault."

Theresa then asked me if it was okay for her to tell Guide One about the rape. She felt that it was important for him to know what had happened so the three of us could talk about what to do next. Theresa's belief in me gave me the courage to want to speak my truth again. I told her I wanted to tell him. I sat next to Theresa, with her holding my hands as I told Guide One what I had just told her.

He came over to me, cupped my chin in his hand, looked me in the eye, and said, "Marie, I am so sorry all this has happened to you. I had no idea your father was hurting you in that way. I will call the police."

I begged them not to call the police. I was afraid of what would happen to me if the police took my father's word over mine. I knew my mother would not support me. I was afraid of what my father would do to me if the police did not take me away.

Theresa suggested an alternative: contacting Child Protective Services (CPS). Theresa explained to me that she could call CPS to explain the physical abuse suffered by my mother and me by my father. "They will send a social worker out to investigate. The investigation would most likely lead to you being taken away from your parents and moved out of your house to live someplace else, or if your mother wants to leave too, they will find a place for you, your mother, and your sister to live. Marie, your mother may be too afraid to leave your father. It is likely your mother will support your father's story since she did not stand with you when you told her he raped you. Are you prepared for the possibility that it may be your word against both of your parents?"

What Theresa and Guide One was telling me scared me a little. No one had ever told me that leaving my parents was an option, but their words were giving me hope, hope for a place to live free of sexual attacks, physical attacks, demoralizing surroundings, and fear. Their words gave me hope that there was a safer place for me and my sister to live away from our parents. Their words gave me permission and strength to seek an alternative way of life without my parents. I was slightly afraid of the unknown, but I thought anyplace had to be better than living in the same house with my father. I had to go with my gut.

I asked Guide One and Theresa to help me contact CPS to start the process of getting help for me to get away from my father, hoping that my mother might seek help too. A few telephone calls resulted in arrangements being made for a social worker to meet me at Theresa's house in the morning. Instead of going to school, I was to go to Theresa's, where the social worker would be waiting to help me. I was told not to bring any of my belongings other than what I would normally bring to school. I was told not to say anything to anyone, especially my mother, about the meeting.

That night at home was scary and sad for me. I was scared that my father would somehow find out about the planned meeting with the social worker. I was afraid that the social worker would believe my parents, leaving me with them to suffer whatever punishment my father deemed appropriate. I was afraid of the unknown. I was sad thinking that I might not see my mother and sister again.

My last night on Gotham Street was the loneliest and saddest night of my life, yet I understood that my family was not available to me and that my mother was unable to help me. I understood that if I wanted a better life, I had to help myself.

Chapter Three

Path to Foster Care

Theresa was the only person in her house when I arrived the next morning. Her kids had left for school; Guide One was at work. Theresa told me that she thought it would be easier for me if I did not have to worry about others being around to overhear my conversation with the social worker.

"Cindy said to tell you she will miss you. She hopes you can write or call her to let her know where you are. Please keep our telephone number so you can call me to let me know how you are doing. Guide One also wants to know where you end up living. He wants you to know he will check in with me to see how you are doing and where you end up."

Tears started to form in my eyes, sadness welling inside of me because I knew I would not see my friends again. I knew I would not see Guide One again. He was gone. I would never get the chance to thank him for guiding me to safety, to thank him for helping me believe I was strong enough to break away from my abusive father.

Theresa asked me if I was nervous. I told her that I was more afraid than nervous, afraid of not knowing what was going to happen next, especially worried that I might have to continue living with my parents. Theresa did her best to keep me calm, telling me funny stories about her youngest kids and asking me about school.

Finally, the female social worker arrived after introducing herself. She explained to me that she was going to ask me several questions about what it was like living at home with my father, mother, and sister. She told me that some of the questions might be uncomfortable for me.

"If you ever feel you need a break from the questions, let me know. We can take a break anytime you need. Just know the questions I ask you will make it easier for me to decide the best way to help you. Do you have any questions before we start?"

I shook my head. I began to feel empowered as I unburdened myself of the secrets that I had held inside for the past twelve to eighteen months: my father's drug use in our house alone and with strangers, the increase in fights between my father and mother, my father's physical assaults on my mother, my father's physical and sexual assaults on me. I felt that most of the interview questions were about the physical and sexual assaults against me, questions that were uncomfortable to answer when the social worker would ask for specifics:

- How long has your father been using drugs? Does your mother take drugs with him?
- How long has your father been hitting your mother? Did he ever hit your sister?
- Do you remember how old you were when your father first hit you?
- Where was your sister when your father and mother would fight?
- When and where did your father first sexually assault you?
- Were you naked during the assaults?
- Was your father naked during the assaults?
- Tell me what your father did to you the first time he sexually assaulted you.
- How many times did your father sexually assault you?
- What did he make you do to him, if anything, during the sexual assaults?
- Would he threaten to hurt you if you told anyone? Did you tell anyone? If so, when?

My feelings of empowerment began to manifest into feelings of guilt as I again began to question why I had not been able to fight my father off me during his attacks, why I had not told my mother sooner about the sexual assaults. The social worker must have noticed the change in my demeanor as I started to pull guilt inward, my body physically tightening as I answered her questions.

She said to me, "You did nothing wrong. These questions are to help me understand the activities in your house, the frequency and types of abuse you have experienced. The more I know about you and your family, the more it helps me make decisions about the best path forward for you. It will also make it easier to make recommendations to the judge."

I thought, *Judge?* I asked the social worker, "Are we going to court?"

She said, "You may have to sit in a courtroom, where a judge will want to question you and your parents to help him make a decision about where you should live. A judge might decide it's okay for you to live with your mother and sister, but you will not be able to live with your father."

"Good. That's what I want. I do not ever want to live with my father again, and I think my mother would leave my father too if she had someplace to live with me and my sister, someplace where we can be safe away from his abuse."

"Joannes, for now, the focus is to get you somewhere safe. Where your mother and sister will live is not my concern today."

When the social worker finished asking me questions, she told me that she was going to drive me to a facility where I would stay until a meeting date could be scheduled with a judge who would make the decision of where I should live.

"Can we go to my house first so I can say goodbye to my mother and sister and get some of my things?"

"I'm sorry, Joannes. You will not be going back to your house for anything. You cannot be anywhere near your house or your parents until the court decides what the next steps will be to make sure you and your sister are safe. I will make arrangements to get your belongings to you."

I started to cry. I did not realize that I would not get to say goodbye to my mother and sister before being taken away. I began to regret starting the process of getting help. I was giving up my home with my mother and sister. I was leaving my friends, my school. I was giving up everything important to me to escape my father's abuse. It did not seem fair that I was having to give up everything. I naively thought that my father would be taken away from our house instead of me, leaving me to stay with my mother, allowing her and me to talk to CPS about our options to live somewhere without my father.

However, my mother did not have the strength to leave my father. She did not have the strength to defend herself or me from my father. She did not have the strength to believe me when I told her I had been raped by my father. I know my mother loved me; she simply did not have the confidence or power to imagine her life without my father. I had to be strong for myself and hope that my mother would eventually follow.

The guidance and support I received from Guide One and Theresa helped me gain confidence in myself. Their support gave me the strength I needed to take the steps to protect myself when my mother was unable to protect me.

MacLaren Hall[1]

I sat quietly in the front seat of the car, listening to the social worker explain to me the place she was taking me to, MacLaren Hall, a temporary spot for me to live until a judge would make the decision for my long-term living arrangements. She told me that I would be around kids of all ages, kids going through the same circumstances as me, who needed a safe place to live.

I asked, "How long will I be at MacLaren Hall?"

"It usually takes three to four weeks before a court date can be scheduled with a judge. A judge needs to study your case based on information I will provide. The judge may also request that your parents appear in court before he decides where you will live. Our goal is to find you a foster home quickly so you can return to school."

I was not sure what a foster home was, so I asked, "Is a foster home a place I will live with more kids?"

"Yes, a foster home is a private home of people who have volunteered to take care of kids who need a place to live. Foster volunteers are usually parents themselves who may have their own children, or they may only take care of foster children. Each foster home is different when it comes to the age and number of children."

"When do you think I will get my clothes and stuff?"

"I will be going to your house after I drop you off to talk to your parents. I will let them know you are okay and also let them know the next steps they have to take with the court to finalize what happens next. I will collect some clothes and personal items for you and then bring them to you."

---

1 Institution for kids run by the Department of Probation, not the state social service agency because most of the children's parents were in the jail system.

I sat silently for the rest of the ride, thinking about what was going to happen to me next, wondering if where I would be living would be close enough for my mother to visit me, hoping that my mother would want to visit me. I was afraid of the unknown but more afraid that I would somehow end up back at home with my father.

Finally, the social worker stopped the car in front of a long concrete building with windows running the length of it. It looked more like a hospital than someplace children would live. Suddenly, I was fearful and nervous as I reached to grab my backpack to follow the social worker through the door entrance into the unknown. We were greeted by a woman who led us into a big room to a table with several chairs around it. This room did not feel like a classroom; there was nothing else in it but this big table with chairs. It felt empty. I felt empty.

I sat listening to the social worker explain my circumstances to the MacLaren woman until I became distracted by the continuous loud sounds of kids playing, screaming from somewhere outside of this lonely room. This place was nosier than any school I had attended. I sat quietly with my loneliness, feeling abandoned and afraid of the unknown I was about to be delivered into. I was slowly losing confidence in my decision to leave my parents. Instead of confidence, I felt myself feeling afraid of the unknown, afraid of being delivered to a building with no escape to await my fate in the hands of complete strangers, locked away from my mother and sister. I felt like I was being punished for my father's crime against me when it should be my father going to jail, not me.

The social worker finally finished her review with the MacLaren woman and prepared to leave, telling me that she would drop my belongings off at the front office by the end of the day. Then she would see me again in a couple of weeks when it was time to see the judge. The MacLaren woman told me that she would deliver my belongings to me as soon as they arrived. In the meantime, she wanted to show me around the general area and classrooms. We exited the big empty room onto a large blacktop area where kids of all ages were sitting at concrete picnic tables, running around, playing basketball and other games that involved a lot of screaming. I was not in the mood to jump into activities with a bunch of kids, so I was relieved when the MacLaren woman told me she would take me to the dormitory to show me where I would put my belongings and where I would share sleeping quarters with girls my age.

We entered a building on the other side of the blacktop. The inside looked like a school gym filled with more kids, some running around, some dancing on a stage, being silly, some sitting quietly, playing games on the same concrete picnic tables we had passed outside. It was loud and hectic. I was beginning to wonder if there would be anyplace quiet in this facility. I was starting to feel slightly claustrophobic, thinking about being confined to a blacktop area and gym with so many other kids around. There did not seem to be enough space for all the kids I was seeing, I began to wonder if there would be anyplace to be alone. I felt like I was walking through a lockdown area where everyone had to stay bunched together to be in the eyeline of the few adults standing on the sidelines, watching the chaos, so I asked what was going on in here. The woman told me this was the indoor recreation area, where most of the kids liked to hang out instead of being stuck in their dormitory rooms. I was not in the mood to make friends. I just wanted a quiet place to rest and think about what happened today.

The dormitory was a long hallway with rooms on each side of the hall. Each room had two sets of bunk beds with two lockers at the end of the bunks. My bed would be a lower bunk. There was no television, the walls were bare, and there was nothing cozy about this room, which felt like a jail cell. The woman told me that I could keep my backpack with me or lock it in a locker that would be mine to store my stuff during my stay. She left me after showing me the bathrooms and shower areas. I returned to my dorm room, where I lay on my assigned lower bunk bed. Feeling lonely, I started to cry because I was afraid of the unknown, hoping that wherever the judge was going to send me would be a better place to live, a place with fewer kids than MacLaren Hall.

I must have cried myself to sleep because I was awakened by someone shaking my bunk bed, talking to me.

"Hi, new girl. I am one of your roommates. My name is Becky. What is your name?"

I replied, "My name is Joannes."

Becky smiled at me and then asked me if I wanted to go with her to the cafeteria to have lunch. She explained that meals were served at the same time every day. "If you miss lunch, it will be dinnertime before you get to eat again, so you need to eat now if you are hungry."

I got out of my bunk bed to follow my new friend, who led me to the cafeteria. I was not in the mood to talk, so I just listened and followed as Becky told me about the different areas we passed, which seemed to differ only based on the ages of the kids. Every alcove, bench, platform, and blacktop area was filled with kids of all ages running, screaming, and playing, without any apparent supervision.

MacLaren looked like a school but lacked the organization of the schools I had attended, unlike my junior high school, where groups of students huddled in organized groups with their friends talking, shooting basketballs into hoops, or trying to complete homework before their next class started. This place was frantic, with hordes of kids overseen by a few adults.

My early days at MacLaren were spent hanging out in the only quiet places I could find, the library or on my bunk bed, reading to be alone and to escape having to interact with any of the other kids. I did not have the energy or desire to be involved in the constant activity of what seemed like hundreds of kids of all ages playing, screaming, and running all day, nonstop, until dinnertime.

One night Becky encouraged me to join her with some other kids who were closer to our age. We would gather for movie nights or listen to music in the auditorium. Listening to music and dancing to music was my happy place, reminding me of the good times when I used to enjoy dancing at home with my mother. In time, the music motivated me to join the other kids who had jumped up on the auditorium stage to dance until it was time to return to our dormitory rooms to crawl into our bunk beds to fall asleep, listening to whispered conversations or someone crying themselves to sleep, myself included.

Other than Becky, I do not recall the names of any of the other kids I met while I was at MacLaren Hall, probably because I did not make much effort to make friends because I was sad and worried about how long I was going to be in this loud yet lonely place. Not knowing where I was going to live, who I was going to live with, filled me with regret about my decision to leave home. I wondered if the loneliness I was feeling would ever go away.

It is strange to feel so lonely when surrounded by people, but none of the people here with me at MacLaren Hall could replace my mother or my sister. I held onto the hope that my mother missed me too and would find the strength to leave my father once the social worker let her know about other living options. I knew I could never return home to my mother if my father was living in the same house.

Meeting with a Judge

Weeks, months passed at MacLaren. Time seemed like it had stopped. Many days were filled with boredom and/or sadness, days when I thought, *This is as good as my life is going, get stuck here with all the other abandoned children*, feeling myself slipping in and out of deep sadness.

I missed my mother and sister. I missed my friends. I missed my school. I missed the privacy of my own bedroom. I missed being able to shower and eat when I wanted to instead of having to do these activities at a scheduled time every day.

Finally, the day arrived when one of the staff members told me that my social worker would be coming to pick me up the next day to go meet with a judge. I was told to make sure I had clean clothes to wear and be ready when the social worker came to pick me up at 8:00 a.m. I was nervous thinking about talking to the judge, but I was also excited thinking I might be closer to going home with my mother.

I did not sleep well during the night, thinking about the possible scenarios that awaited me. The judge might not believe what my father did to me and decide to send me back home to live with both of my parents. He might tell my mother that I could go live with her if she made other living arrangements away from my father, or I might be going to live with strangers. I was afraid of what was going to happen next, but I was also looking forward to seeing my mother even if it was going to be in a courtroom.

The social worker was already waiting for me when I stepped into the lobby at 8:00 a.m. "Good morning, Joannes. You look nice for our meeting with the judge this morning. How are you doing?"

I told her that I was nervous but also excited to see my mother. We spent the driving time to the courthouse discussing what my time had been like in MacLaren.

As we pulled into the courthouse parking lot, my social worker turned off her car, turned to me, and said, "I want to talk to you about what you can expect when we enter the courtroom. There will be two tables in front of the judge's desk. You and I will sit at one table, and your parents will probably be sitting at the other table together."

I swear that my breath left my body when I heard the words "your parents." I thought I would never have to see my father again after what he had done to me. My parents together for this meeting also confirmed what I dreaded—my mother was still with my father.

I asked, "My parents? My father is here? My mother is still with my father? Why does he have to be here? Will I have to talk to him?"

"Joannes, Child Protective Services has no influence on whether or not your parents stay together. Our job is to keep you safe with or without your parents. This meeting is to help the judge decide what is best for you, and that decision may not allow for you to live with your mother if she continues to live with your father."

"I am afraid of being in the same room with my father. I am afraid of my father."

"Joannes, you will be safe. I will be by your side the entire time, and the judge will have your father removed from the courtroom if he does not obey the judge's rules."

"All right. I should be okay as long as you are next to me. I do not want to talk to my father."

The social worker and I walked through the halls of a large building, opening the double doors to a small courtroom where a judge was sitting at a long conference table that faced two smaller empty tables. He looked up from the papers he was reading to greet us, asking us to sit at the table to his left. Then he approached me, reaching out his hand to me. I thought he was going to shake my hand, but he gently took my hand into his, holding it as he looked me in the eye to tell me his name, and then asked me for my name. His simple act of looking directly into my eyes while holding my hand comforted me.

"My name is Joannes. My family calls me Marie to avoid confusion since I am named after my mother."

He asked, "What would you prefer I call you during today's meeting?"

"Joannes, please. My friends know me as Joannes."

"Joannes it is. Now, Joannes, do you have any questions about what we will be doing here today?"

"My social worker told me both of my parents are going to be here so you can ask them questions. Will I have to talk to my father? I don't want to talk to him or be near him."

"Joannes, you do not have to talk to either of your parents if you do not want to talk to them. You can look at me or your social worker the entire time."

"Will I get to talk to my mother?"

"Joannes, the purpose of this meeting is to help me understand what is going to be the safest and best place for you to live. I will be asking you and your parents a lot of questions about what happened in your home before you were removed by CPS. If, at the end of our meeting, I feel it is safe for you to talk with your mother, we will arrange for you to have some alone time with her."

"Okay," I said. I felt some excitement knowing I would be able to talk to my mother alone.

"Then let us get started," the judge said as he returned to his desk. "I will ask the deputy to bring your parents into the courtroom. You get comfortable at your table and feel free to let your social worker know if you have any questions or need anything."

I sat quietly at the conference table next to my social worker, feeling nervous and worried about what was going to happen next. Several minutes passed before the double doors from the hallway opened, with a uniformed deputy leading the way into the courtroom, with my mother and father close behind him. My father had his arm entwined around my mother's left arm as if he were leading her into the courtroom.

I felt disappointment seeing my father with my mother. I guess I had held onto the hope that they would enter separately, signaling that my mother had left my father and was here to take me home with her. I had hoped that my mother had gained the strength to leave my father. Instead, all I saw was fatigue and nervousness in her face and her body. I wanted to make eye contact with my mother, but she looked straight ahead as my father guided her to the table the deputy had led them to sit side by side.

I kept my eyes on my mother, knowing she would eventually look around the courtroom to find me. We were able to make eye contact right after she settled into the chair the deputy had pulled out for her to sit on at the end closest to the table where I was sitting. My eyes welled with tears when my mother finally made eye contact with me. I smiled at her, and she smiled back at me.

"Hi, Mom," I pantomimed with my lips.

"Hi, Marie," she whispered back to me.

Then I noticed that my father was looking at me, smiling, waving his fingers at me in a fanlike manner like I was a small child whose attention he was trying to get in a playful manner. His actions made me furious. He was acting as though everything was okay between us. Being in the same proximity of my father sickened and terrified me. I quickly looked away, eyes forward, toward the judge, who had begun to address my parents.

"Good morning, Mrs. Boman, Mr. Boman. As you know, we are here today to decide what will be the safest living arrangements for your daughter Joannes. There are a few items we need to address before we discuss options. Let us start with you, Mr. Boman. Are you currently employed?"

My father replied, "I am, Your Honor. I am a truck driver."

"Are you employed full-time?"

"I am not, Your Honor. Work is slow at the moment, but we get by with the money I do make and my wife's disability checks."

"Mr. Boman, I see you are on probation for a past violation that involved drug possession preceded by a petty theft incident. I am concerned about your ability to support your family. Are you concerned about your ability to support your wife?"

"Your Honor, being employed is a requirement of my probation status. I drive all long-haul trips that are available to me. Sometimes there can be a several-weeks gap between jobs."

"Mr. Boman, you have already stated that you and your wife have had to depend on her disability checks, which do not seem adequate to support your wife, you, and your youngest daughter. Is your youngest daughter currently living with you and Mrs. Boman?"

My father smiled and replied, "Yes, Your Honor. Our youngest daughter does live with us. She is in school this morning. I am sure she is enjoying her schoolwork and playground time like most kids in second grade."

I barely paid attention as the conversation between the judge and my father continued. I needed to avoid the frustration and anger brewing inside me, listening to my father make excuse upon excuse about why he was not able to work full-time, even citing that he had to take care of my mother. I wanted to say out loud, "Since when have you ever taken care of Mom?" I began to worry that the judge would not see through my father's charade of pleasantries. I was hoping the judge would recognize that the generous smile and jovial manner my father was exuding was a mask hiding the flaws of his character.

Finally, the judge asked my father in a direct and firm manner, "Mr. Boman, I am hearing a lot of why you have not been able to work, but I do not sense you have taken any steps to improve your job situation, which would include being able to take care of your family without depending on your wife's disability checks."

My father attempted to make a rebuttal comment until the judge cut him off, saying he wanted to ask my mother a few questions. "How are you today, Mrs. Boman?"

"I am okay, Your Honor, a little nervous sitting in a courtroom," my mother said with a faint smile.

"Well, I think all of us are a little nervous, as we should be, considering we will be discussing what is best for the welfare of your eldest daughter."

My mother simply nodded, with her eyes focused on the judge.

"Mrs. Boman, do you have any questions for me before we begin discussing this case?"

"None that I can think of at this time, Your Honor."

"All right. Then let us begin by reviewing the circumstances that led to Joannes being removed from your home. Mr. and Mrs. Boman, the information I have reviewed about your case is from reports provided by Child Protective Services based on information provided by the doctor who examined your eldest daughter, neighbors who know your family and will attest to the acts of physical abuse they have witnessed Mr. Boman inflict upon Joannes and you, Mrs. Boman. I have also reviewed the arrest records of Mr. Boman, which show a pattern of drunk driving and drug possession.

"Your eldest daughter has provided details of several incidents when she suffered beatings from Mr. Boman, who, on several occasions, used a belt, often leaving welt marks on the lower half of her body, sometimes causing bleeding welts and/or bruises that required her to cover up with long pants to hide the wounds. Mr. Boman would often inflict violent backhand slaps across his daughter's face for minor infractions such as talking back to him or Mrs. Boman. Mr. Boman has grabbed his daughter by her hair to drag her out of her bed late at night into the kitchen to make her wash the dinner dishes on the occasions she did not wash the dishes before going to bed. Social Services has confirmed this with a friend of the family who lived in your household for several months and was witness to the physical attacks inflicted upon Joannes and Mrs. Boman. This friend intervened on several occasions to defuse the violent altercations.

"Mr. Boman's abusive behavior escalated to inappropriate touching of his eldest daughter's genitalia while she was asleep in her bed at night. On several occasions, Mr. Boman forced his daughter to touch his penis until erect, at which time he would rape her in her bed in the middle of the night when Mrs. Boman and their younger daughter were asleep in separate bedrooms. Mr. Boman would threaten his daughter with violence if she attempted to scream, often applying pressure with his hand and forearm to his daughter's mouth or throat, threatening to 'beat the shit out of you and your mother if you wake anyone up with your screaming.'"

The judge stopped reading and paused to look at my father, who was looking down at the table, before turning to my mother to ask, "Mrs. Boman, on any occasion, did you ever hear cries or screams coming from Joannes's bedroom in the middle of the night?"

"No, Your Honor, I did not. I have been on antidepressants and other medications since my stroke, which make me sleep pretty soundly."

"Did your daughter ever tell you that your husband was coming into her room at night while you were asleep?"

"One time Marie told me she was awakened during the night by her daddy, who was sitting on the edge of her bed, touching himself in the crotch area, looking at her. She said she screamed when she 'saw a man sitting on her bed.' Then she realized it was her daddy, who quickly left the room when she screamed. I told her Daddy was probably drunk and didn't realize he was in her bedroom instead of our bedroom."

"Did you ask Mr. Boman why he was in your daughter's bedroom in the middle of the night, sitting on her bed while fondling himself?"

"Yes, Your Honor. He told me he did not go into Marie's bedroom, that she was just making up lies because she was probably mad at him for making her do her chores."

"Mrs. Boman, can you tell me what your reaction was when your daughter told you your husband had been going into her bedroom at night to rape her?"

"I thought she was making up stories because Marie and her daddy are always fighting about something, I thought Marie was just acting out for attention. I asked my husband if he was going into Marie's room drunk again. He told me no. Then I asked him why he thought Marie would be so mad at him to accuse him of rape. He told me she was just trying to cause trouble between me and him to hide the fact that she was probably having sex with a male friend who was living at our house for a while."

"Mrs. Boman, did you even consider that your daughter was telling you the truth about being raped by her father?"

"No, Your Honor. I guess I thought Marie was just trying to get even with her father because he was always picking at her or giving her belt whippings for talking back to him."

"Did you ever consider that your husband suggesting your twelve-year-old daughter was having sex with an adult male whom you and Mr. Boman allowed to live in your house was suspicious considering your daughter had just told you her father had raped her?"

My mother turned toward my father as if she wanted him to answer the question for her.

"Mrs. Boman, please answer my question."

"Our friend moved out shortly after Marie said her daddy raped her. I guess I thought my husband told him to move out of our house because he was having sex with Marie."

"Did you attempt to talk to your daughter to ask her if she had been having sex with the adult male living in your house?"

My mother sat quiet with her head hung low, avoiding eye contact with the judge before replying, "No, I did not talk to Marie about having sex with anyone. She did not come to me to talk about him after he moved out, and I knew my husband had handled the situation. There was so much arguing and fighting going on in our house between my husband and Marie. I just wanted it to stop, but I didn't know what to think or what to do about it."

The judge paused simply, looking at my mother with dismay before he addressed my father. "Mr. Boman, why did you allow your friend to stay in your home if you thought he was sexually involved with your eldest daughter?"

It was obvious that my father was not ready for this question when he kept his head down, trying to avoid making eye contact with the judge before replying, "Your Honor, I do not recall suggesting to my wife that our daughter was having sex with our house guest."

"What I am hearing you say, Mr. Boman, is that your daughter is not telling the truth and your wife is not telling the truth. Do you expect me to believe you are the only one telling the truth about the events that took place in your home?"

"Your Honor, I know I have no influence on what you think or the decisions you will make about my family. I only know what I have said here in this courtroom today is what I remember doing and not doing."

Deflection and lying—just a couple of my father's unsavory personality traits. Any hope I had of living with my mother and sister slowly faded away as I listened to my mother accuse me of lying about being raped by my father. Hearing her say that she thought I was making up stories to get even with my father made me feel unloved and ashamed. My mother's words hurt me deeply. Sadness filled every pore of my body as I realized I was alone, alone in this battle to get away from my abusive father.

My mind went numb until I heard the judge call my name.

"Joannes, how are you doing?"

I started crying as soon as I heard the judge's question. I could only sob, "Not good."

He replied, "It's okay if you are feeling upset or even a bit scared right now. You have been through a lot. You are going to be okay. We're almost done here. Mrs. Boman, do you have any thoughts about what should be done to keep Joannes safe?" My father started to answer for my mother, but the judge held up his hand to my father, saying, "I want to hear from Mrs. Boman."

My mother paused for a minute or two before replying through teary eyes, "I think Marie needs to live somewhere else. I don't think I can take care of her, and I don't think the constant fighting between her and her father is good for her or me."

Hearing my mother say that she thought I should live someplace else felt like a punch to my gut. I had no home to return to with my mother because she had settled, settled for a life with my father. I realized that she had chosen my father over me a long time ago; I simply did not realize this truth until I heard her say I should live somewhere else. Looking back now, I think my mother requested I be sent somewhere else to live because she knew. She knew what my father was doing to me, but she did not know how to make him stop. How could she when she was unable to protect herself?

The judge did not ask my father for his input about whether or not I should return home to live. Instead, he turned toward our table and looked at my social worker, nodding toward her as if they had a secret. The social worker put her hand on mine and told me everything was going to be okay. Then the judge began to explain to my parents that I would not be returning home to live with them.

"Mr. Boman, you have demonstrated that you are not capable of maintaining steady work to support your family, a symptom of your excessive drinking and drug use, which appears to be habits you are not willing to change. Your violence against your family is an unfortunate consequence of your drinking and drug abuse, often putting your wife and your eldest daughter in danger. Mrs. Boman, although I can sympathize with your circumstances, I cannot ignore your responsibility in keeping your daughter safe. It seems you have forgotten Joannes is a child, a child who, by all circumstances, is trying to survive in an unstable home that lacks parental protection or guidance."

The judge turned to me. "Joannes, I am sorry you had to go through this process today, but know you are a strong young girl who has done nothing wrong—except maybe ditching school." The judge smiled at me when he said this, his attempt to lighten the heaviness of the truth that hung in the room. "You have your entire life ahead of you. Know it is my job now, along with your social worker, to make sure you are placed in a safe home where you can continue going to school."

The judge continued, "Mr. and Mrs. Boman, I am issuing a court order making your daughter Joannes a ward of the state, where she will be placed into foster care until you are able to provide a safe home environment free of alcohol and drug use. I am also recommending social services make quarterly visits to your home for the next year to ensure the safety of your youngest daughter. In addition, Mr. Boman must provide proof to this court of his full-time employment and get help for his alcohol and drug addictions, or this court may be forced to remove your youngest daughter from your home. Mr. Boman, it is my hope that you will actively seek help for your addictions to become a better father to your daughters and a better husband for your wife."

I cried. I felt relief that I did not have to live with my father, but I also felt great sadness that I was not going to be able to live with my mother and sister. I never even got to say goodbye to my sister.[2]

---

2   My sister was placed into foster care shortly after I left home. Her first placement was with the Fergusons for a very short time while social services found a permanent foster home for her. She could not be placed with me at the Fergusons because they were only licensed to care for teenagers; she was only eight years old at the time. My sister lived in the foster care system, eventually returning to live with our parents.

My First Foster Home

I spent the next few weeks at MacLaren Hall thinking about the court proceeding, wondering if anyone believed that my father had raped me. Why didn't the judge sentence my father to jail for raping me? Was it because there were no witnesses? Was it because as bad as my parents' relationship was, the judge recognized that my mother needed my father to support her and my sister, or was it because that was how child incestuous abuse was handled in the 1970s—simply remove the child from the danger, have everyone act as if the sexual assault did not happen and get on with living their lives as if nothing bad had occurred, that time will pass and everyone will forget and do better except the victim? I would never forget.

I did not want to be forever burdened with the pain of physical abuse, the shame of being raped, the betrayal of my parents. I made a conscious decision not to be defined by my circumstances. I felt confident that I was going to do better now that I was going to be safe. I worked to suppress the memories that I had been raped by my father. I learned to push my feelings deep down inside, eventually becoming comfortable in my own skin, knowing that my father could not hurt me again.

Time passed slowly for me at MacLaren Hall after the judge had deemed me a "ward of the state." I spent my days wondering when my social worker would return to pick me up to take me to a home where I would meet strangers who could possibly be my future foster parents.

I was very apprehensive about living with strangers who would get to decide if they wanted me to live with them. I wondered if I would have any say in where I would live, or was I simply expected to live wherever the social worker delivered me? I felt abandoned, sad, and fearful of what living with people I did not know would be like, wondering what it meant to be a foster child. Would I be treated differently because I was a foster child? I had no idea what to expect, yet I allowed myself to feel some excitement because I would be leaving MacLaren Hall to live in a house. I was looking forward to returning to a normal school schedule, where I could make new friends.

My social worker told me a little bit about my potential new foster parents as we drove to their house to meet them. "They are a nice young couple who have always wanted to foster a child but wanted to own their own home first and wait until their two young daughters had passed the toddler stage."

As I listened to the social worker describe this wonderful family, I could not help but wonder why a young couple who had two kids of their own would want a strange kid living in their house. Whatever their reason, I was beginning to feel thankful that there were people who were willing to help children who needed a home.

The social worker drove her car into a neighborhood filled with houses that looked new, newly painted with big green lawns, a neighborhood that looked like everyone worked together to keep their street beautiful. I got a little scared and nervous when the car stopped in front of one of the nice houses. Suddenly, the recognition that I was going to live with complete strangers overwhelmed me to the point of tears. The social worker talked me through the process, noting that I would not have to live with this family if I felt that it would not be a good fit for me. She told me to keep an open mind and ask any questions I wanted to ask, acknowledging that my feelings and opinions on where I would live were just as important as the opinions of the foster parents wanting me to live with them.

The front door of the house opened before we stepped on the porch to knock on the door. Standing in the doorway was a young couple greeting us with bright smiles on their faces.

"Hello. You must be Joannes. I'm Bill, and this is my wife, Cathy."

I replied with a meek hello.

Cathy said, "Welcome to our home, your new home." Then she led me into the house, with Bill and the social worker following close behind.

I was enjoying the bright light that came in through the windows, highlighting the clean, organized living space as Cathy guided us into the living room, where there were snacks waiting for us on the table. This was a cozy home. It reminded me of Dunaway Drive, the only home where my parents, I, and my sister had enjoyed light, laughter, and love before we were split apart by the tragic events that delivered me to this house today.

Cathy and Bill told me that they had been looking forward to meeting me and that their girls were so excited to get a big sister that they had worn themselves out and needed to be put down for a nap.

Cathy said, "Which is better for us because Bill and I wanted some time alone with you before the girls kidnap you."

Big sister? I felt weird thinking about these little girls who were going to call me their sister. It did not seem right. I felt like I would be betraying my sister if I were a big sister to these little girls who were strangers to me.

Sad reality check: it had been a while since I had felt like a big sister to my little sister. We had not seen each other in months, and even before I was taken out of our home, I had developed feelings of resentment toward my sister, wondering how she had avoided being a victim of my father's physical abuse. What was wrong with me that made my father want to hurt me and my mother not help me? It seemed to me that my mother would try to protect my sister while leaving me to fight the battles with my father by myself. Of course, my sister did not deserve my resentment; she was only seven years old when I was removed from our home.

The social worker and my new foster parents chatted for a few minutes together while I sat alone in the living room until the social worker came to tell me she was leaving. She wished me good luck in my new home and handed me her contact card, telling me to call her anytime if I needed her.

Cathy and Bill joined me in the living room, where we sat for a while, with them asking me how my time was at MacLaren, what school had been like while I was there, small talk until they asked if I had any questions about living with them.

I really did not know what to ask since I had never been in a situation like this before, so I asked, "Will I have my own bedroom?"

They both chuckled and said, "Yes, yes. I guess we should have shown you your bedroom and the bathroom first so you can put your stuff away."

The bedroom they took me to was next to their daughters', across the hall from Cathy and Bill's bedroom; I would be sharing a bathroom with the girls. Cathy and Bill left me alone to unpack my small suitcase while they went to wake up their daughters.

I felt like I was in another world. I was happy to be out of MacLaren Hall. I was glad to be away from my father. It felt good to know I now had a safe bedroom to sleep in by myself, but I found my eyes filling with tears as I wondered when I would see my mother again.

I was not left to wallow in my sorrow for very long because I heard the voices of little girls heading toward the door of my room—"Mommy, Daddy, where is our big sister?" It was time for me to be part of a family again.

I quickly felt at ease and safe with Cathy and Bill, who checked in with me frequently to ask how I was feeling if I needed anything. I enjoyed playing with their young daughters, who were cute and seemingly infatuated with me, always wanting to be around me.

My time with this family was very brief. I lived with them during the summer between my seventh- and eighth-grade school years. I had just settled into living with this family when the social worker came to visit with the news that she would be taking me to live in a long-term foster home. I cried because I had just begun to feel safe and relaxed living with this family. More importantly, I felt like they truly cared about me. Hearing that I was going to be moved to a different foster home made me feel like I had done something wrong or that there was something that Cathy and Bill did not like about me.

I asked, "Why do I have to go live at another foster home? Did I do something wrong?"

Cathy immediately came to sit next to me. "Oh no, Joannes. You have done nothing wrong. Bill, the girls, and I all loved having you live with us. You are moving to a home where you can live until you are old enough to take care of yourself."

"Why can't I stay with you until I am old enough to live on my own?"

"Because Bill and I did not sign up to be long-term foster parents. We were not sure we would be able to foster for a long period with our girls being so young."

"But I can help you with the girls like I've been doing. I can be your helper for anything you need."

Tears formed in Cathy's eyes. She just looked at me as if she did not know what to say.

Bill came over to sit on the other side of me. "Joannes, Cathy and I did not know what to expect as foster parents. That is why we wanted to try short-term fostering first. After meeting you, we have come to realize how difficult it is going to be to have kids like you removed from our house to live elsewhere. It is heartbreaking to become attached to you and then have to send you away to another home, but we know you will do well wherever you go because you are a smart girl."

What I heard was *Joannes, we do not want you living with us anymore because we only want our daughters living in our house. We do not like you enough to have you live with us until you are eighteen years old.*

The social worker interrupted. "Joannes, I know this is upsetting for you now, but you are moving to a nice foster home with kids your own age, where you will be able to live until you graduate from high school."

I spent my last night with my first foster family feeling sad, disappointed, and somewhat afraid, afraid of what the next foster home would be like. I was going to miss Cathy's and Bill's kind, caring demeanors. Living with them had been very peaceful. Living with them felt like home.

I was packed and ready to go when the social worker came to pick me up the next morning to drive me to the next foster home. Goodbyes were filled with tears. Cathy and Bill asked me to stay in touch with them to let them know how I was doing. I was unable to stay in touch, but their kindness and love for me left an indelible mark on my heart forever.

Forever Foster Home

It is important to note here a symbol of guidance that I was not aware of at the time yet will confirm my belief that I had spirit guides watching over me most of my life. The places and the people I lived with after being placed in the foster care system all contained eight letters: MacLaren, Frenette, and Ferguson. Angel number eight is a sign of being on the right path in your life. It is related to positive thoughts and positive things around you, eliminating negativity from your life, helping you see that life is getting better, see things in a more positive light, build self-confidence, and believe in yourself.

Living with the Frenette family had made me feel that life was getting better. I left them feeling optimistic about moving forward into the unknown. Anything had to be better than the life I would have endured if I lived in a house with my father. Living in safe environments with kind, encouraging adults definitely helped me gain the self-confidence I needed to begin to believe in myself. The positive reinforcement I received from foster parents helped erase the negative messages my father had instilled in my young mind.

The social worker told me we had a short drive[3] from Cathy and Bill's house to meet my new foster parents, a couple who have been foster parents

---

3 At the time, I did not know that my forever foster home was only two miles from the Frenettes' home. Foster parents were not allowed to stay in touch or inquire about the whereabouts of underage foster children, and I was not astute enough to write down their telephone number, if even allowed. I was able to reconnect with the Frenettes fifty years later to thank them and let them know that they had affected me in a profound way. Not surprisingly, their kindness, selflessness, and generosity continued for years, with them caring for many young foster children.

for a few years, starting when they moved from Edinburgh, Scotland, to Canada, where they fostered newborn babies waiting to be adopted. The Fergusons decided to foster teenagers when they moved to California because homes for teenagers were the most underserved foster care resource at the time. The social worker also mentioned that they had two adult children of their own: their daughter, Marlene, who lived with them, and their son, who was in the army.

I was not putting much effort into listening to what the social worker was telling me about this next foster home she was taking me to. I could only think about whether or not I was going to like the next foster parents as much as I liked Cathy and Bill. However, it was admirable to hear that the Ferguson family was dedicated to taking care of teenage foster kids. Foster care is similar to adoptions in the sense that potential parents want the cute young kids they assume have not developed bad behaviors. Often assumptions are made about teenagers being the cause of their removal from home versus the reality of neglect and abuse from a parent or both parents.

I asked, "Is this going to be the last foster home I have to move to, or will I be moving again?"

The social worker told me that this home could be my forever home. Ideally, a forever home is the foster home a teenager will live in until they are eighteen years old or until a family member, if any, is able to take care of them. "Whether or not you stay in this home also depends on you. Think of the Fergusons as your parents. Follow their rules, do well in school, and you will be fine."

Of course, the longevity in a forever home—or any foster home, for that matter—depends on the compatibility of the child with the foster family and other kids living in the home.

In the 1970s (and still today), reaching your eighteenth birthday or aging out of foster care was the court term meaning the foster child was no longer the responsibility of the State of California and no longer a ward of the state, therefore transferring the financial responsibility to the now adult foster to provide for themselves without any preparedness provided by the state to assist with emancipation.

The responsibility of supporting myself as soon as I graduated from high school was a daunting reality presented to all foster teenagers whose focus should be doing well in high school to get a diploma. Fortunately, for today's foster youth, there are many private nonprofit organizations[4] to assist them with their transition from foster care to independence.

When we pulled up to the curb on Van Ruiten Street, I thought, *This looks like a nice house.* It was not as new as the previous foster home, but it looked cozy, with lots of windows on the front of the house, where I could see a man and a woman sitting at a kitchen table. The front door opened as we approached the sidewalk. An older woman in a sky-blue, white-polka-dotted smock dress stood at the front door, waiting to greet us. She was shorter than me, with rich black hair wrapped up into a white hair turban secured with bobby pins.

She smiled at us as she opened the screen door to greet us with a thick Scottish accent. "You must be Joannes. Welcome. I am Christina, but you can call me Mom whenever you're ready. Step inside to meet my husband, Jim—or Dad, if you prefer."

A man who looked old enough to be a grandfather got up from the dining room table, walking toward me with his hand held out to take my hand into his. Winking at me, he said, "Hello, young lady. I hope you call me Dad. Come in, come in." Mr. Ferguson had a gentle demeanor with a twinkle in his eyes; I immediately knew I was going to like him.

I said hello, smiling at both of them, loving the sound of their accents, which were happy and inviting. Mrs. Ferguson was also nice. I could tell she was in charge as she did the introductions and guided us to sit at the same kitchen table they had been sitting at when I spotted them through the louvered windows from the car.

"Sit, sit," Mrs. Ferguson said as she took my suitcase from my hand to set next to a washing machine close to a hallway entry.

Dining room chairs were pulled out from under the table for me and the social worker to sit. Pointing to a glass Pyrex pot sitting on a trivet, Mr. Ferguson asked if we would like some tea. I declined, never having had tea before. I was intimidated by how black it looked steeping on the trivet.

Once we were settled into our chairs, the conversation began between the adults, mostly the social worker summarizing that I needed to register for eighth grade. Mrs. Ferguson assured the social worker that she had already contacted the local junior high school where a couple "of our other

---

4   Examples include CaliforniaCasa.org, Nationalcasagal.org, and Foster Care to Success.

kids are attending," noting that I would start school at Washington Junior High right away.

Mrs. Ferguson turned to me. "Joannes, do you like school?"

"Yes, yes, I do. I miss my friends from my old school though."

"Well, you will make lots of new friends, starting with your foster sisters and brothers, whom you will meet when they get home from school this afternoon."

"How many other kids live here?"

"You bring our total to six. We have three boys who are in high school and two girls. One is a junior in high school. The other is in seventh grade and is the sister to one of the boys." She smiled at me and said, "The girls will be happy that the boys will not outnumber them now that you are here. Our daughter Marlene also lives with us. You will meet her later when gets home from work."

The Fergusons discussed a few more details with the social worker before Mrs. Ferguson told me to grab my suitcase to follow her down the hallway to see the room I would be staying in with the other girls. The social worker followed behind as we walked down the hallway from the kitchen toward the back of the house, passing one bedroom on the left, which was Mr. and Mrs. Ferguson's bedroom, declared "off limits" as we walked by the door. The boys' bedroom was next to the Fergusons'; the girls' bedroom was across the narrow hallway with the bathroom next to it. Mrs. Ferguson pointed out the empty drawers in the dresser that I would share with the other girls as well as the closet that already looked filled with clothes, but I did not have too many clothes to be worried about space.

Mrs. Ferguson pointed to a door that was on the wall opposite the dresser at the foot of the bunk beds. "Marlene's room is just on the other side of that door. Her room and that part of the house is off-limits to you kids. Marlene has a door she can exit onto the patio to get to the front of the house so she does not have to pass through your room."

The boys and girls shared one bathroom, making me wonder how that was going to work if all of us had to get ready for school at the same time. Mrs. Ferguson pointed out that I would be sleeping on the top bunk bed since the other girls had already taken the bottom beds.

"Okay, this is the end of the grand house tour," Mrs. Ferguson declared. "Joannes, why don't you start unpacking while we finish up our meeting? I will come check on you when we're done."

I busied myself putting my clothes away until the Fergusons and the social worker finished up some paperwork. Then Mrs. Ferguson called down the hallway from the kitchen, telling me to come get something to eat.

I sat at the kitchen table between the Fergusons, quietly eating the sandwich Mrs. Ferguson had made for me. Mr. Ferguson asking me a few questions about my stay at MacLaren Hall and my previous foster home. I was very comfortable talking with Mr. Ferguson, who was a man of few words with cheerful gray eyes, an easy smile, and a soft-spoken manner that put me at ease.

Mrs. Ferguson controlled most of the conversation to tell me about my foster siblings, the neighborhood, and the school I would be attending. "Washington Junior High School is within walking distance of the house. I'm sure Tammy will be happy to have a buddy to walk to school with."

Mrs. Ferguson went onto explain the rules of the house to me. "Do well in school, complete your household chores, be home for dinner at 6:00 p.m. or you won't get to eat, and mind your curfew, which, for you, is going to be home by dark. Follow these rules, and you will be free to use your time as you like as long as you let me know where you are going when you leave the house."

Mr. Ferguson faked a stern look, saying to me in a thick Scottish brogue, which I would soon learn was his method of getting our attention (plus, it required good listening skills to interpret what some of the words meant in plain English), "Break any of these rules, and I will have to take off my leather belt to use on your arse." He winked; I smiled.

After I finished my sandwich, Mrs. Ferguson told me that I could leave the table to go unpack. "Go get acquainted with your space before the other kids get home from school."

I was glad to have some time alone to be quiet in this new space that would be my home for the foreseeable future. I was overwhelmed with so many emotions—sad, thinking about missing my mother and sister, wondering when I would see them again; nervous, wondering what it was going to be like living with four older foster siblings; anxious, thinking about attending a new school.

I hopped up onto my top bunk bed, pushing my face into my pillow, crying myself to sleep, wondering if the other foster kids would be nice, hoping that everyone would like me, especially the Fergusons. I really wanted this house to be my forever home if my forever home was going to be a foster home.

Foster Siblings

I was awakened by someone whispering, "Hey, new girl. Joanna. Joanna, wake up."

It took me several seconds to come out of the sleep fog before I realized I was not dreaming, to recall where I was. I opened my eyes to see a girl about my age with shoulder-length dark wavy hair, smiling at me with slight buck teeth and freckles on her cheeks, standing on the bottom bunk bed, putting herself at eye level with me.

"Hi, Joanna. I'm Tammy."

"Hi, Tammy. I'm Joannes." I emphasized the "s," which would be a requirement for the rest of my life whenever meeting people for the first time.

"Oh, JO-ANN-SSSSSS. Sorry."

"It's okay. I'm used to having to repeat or spell my name. It's unusual."

"It's pretty," Tammy said.

I knew I was going to like this girl, who was friendly and full of exuberance. "Thank you," I replied. "Did you just get home from school?"

"Yes, I am usually the first one home because my school, our school, is closer than the high school where the other kids who live here go. Me and my brother were the newest kids here. Now you are the newest. We moved in about three months ago. There are two brothers who were here a few months before us. The eldest girl in the house has lived here the longest. She is a senior in high school."

I asked, "How do you like living here?"

"It's good. This house is much cleaner than the one we lived in before. Plus, Mom and Dad are much nicer than our other foster parents, who used to argue all the time, yell at us kids, and make us do all the housework. Here, we are allowed to do pretty much whatever we want as long as we finish our chores and make sure homework is done before watching television or going outside. We also have to follow the house rules. We are only allowed in our rooms, our bathroom, the kitchen, and the front or back yard. The living room, Dad's den, and their bedrooms and bathroom are off-limits."

"Where's the television?" I asked.

"There is only one television for us to use. The boys usually keep it in their room, or we watch it at the kitchen table together after Dad and Mom are finished with dinner. We girls can have it in our room if we want. It's just easier to watch in the kitchen. Oh, we are not allowed in the kitchen when Dad and Mom are eating dinner. We eat dinner when they are finished."

From what I had seen of the house, the kitchen was the only way to exit the house through the side kitchen door or the front door in the living room. It seemed weird to me that we would not be allowed in the kitchen while the Fergusons had dinner. I was curious to see how this rule would be monitored.

Tammy and I talked until the other kids got home from school. I learned that Tammy and her brother were in foster care because their mother had left, leaving them with their father, who was unable to work and care for them. Their father started drinking heavily, taking his anger out on his kids, physically hurting them, afflicting the most beatings on his son, who would always try to protect his sister. Eventually, their father contacted social services, asking for his kids to be placed into foster care until he could find a job.

I told my story, leaving out the part where I had been raped by my father. I did not want to relive the sexual assaults. Plus, I thought I would eventually forget that I had been raped if I did not talk about it. I was too naive to understand that our bodies hold on to trauma until we acknowledge the stored pain that is in the deepest core of our being until we forgive the offender and, most importantly, forgive ourselves; only then is the burden of guilt lifted.

By the end of my first day in the Fergusons' home, I had heard each of my foster siblings' stories before dinnertime. The teenage brothers had moved to the United States with their father, who owned a car wash somewhere in Los Angeles, where he made them work until social services found out that his sixteen- and seventeen-year-old sons were not enrolled in school nor old enough to be working eight- to ten-hour shifts at the car wash. They did not mind working for their father—they wanted to stay with him—but someone contacted social services to report that their father was using child labor.

The boys did not understand why they could not work; social services had to explain to their father that child labor was not allowed in the United

States, even though they were family. Their father said that he could not afford to take care of his sons if they were not allowed to work at the car wash. The boys came to understand that they had to go to school until they were old enough to get a work permit or graduate from high school. They were placed into foster care, looking forward to attending school, but would still sneak away on weekends to hitchhike or bum rides from friends to go work at their father's car wash.

The eldest foster sibling was a junior in high school. She had been in three foster homes before placement with the Fergusons. Initially, not giving many details about why she was in foster care, she seemed to me to be the most mature in our group, seemingly older than seventeen years with a calm, assured demeanor, as if she were just biding her time in this final foster home before moving onto something better. Her story made me feel so sad for her—losing her mother, betrayed by her father. I could not help comparing our circumstances, recognizing that as much as my mother had hurt me by choosing my father over me, she was still alive and may come to take me home with her someday.

I would come to admire her determination to move beyond her circumstances. She would take extra classes to improve her writing skills, learning how to operate a VariTyper (pre-computers) so she could be a typist for the school newspaper, a skill she would be able to build upon in the future when looking for a job. She was willing to take on any new task or new skill that would help her get a job to support herself as soon as she aged out of foster care. She became a good role model for me, making me recognize that we did not have to wait for social services or an adult figure to show us a path to successfully aging out of foster care. She took every opportunity available to learn and work.

I also met Marlene, the eldest of the Fergusons' two adult children, that first evening when she arrived home from work while we kids were gathered at the kitchen table, eating dinner. Marlene looked older than twenty-seven years, dressed in oversized smock blouses paired with basic black pants, her face framed in horn-rimmed glasses, her hair pulled back in a tight ponytail. Marlene did not smile easily; she almost seemed shy but kind. She seemed to have a good rapport with the older kids, who told me Marlene was nice enough to us, but her loyalty was to her mother.

"Marlene will tell Mom if we do anything wrong. Make sure you never say anything bad about Mom in front of Marlene because she will tell Mom."

It helped to have friendly foster siblings. All of us sharing the trauma of being removed from our homes made it easier for me to settle into this new place, knowing I was going to live with a group of my peers. Even though the circumstances that had brought us together were not ideal, there was a sense of unity among our group that was a positive distraction from our circumstances.

Getting to know each of my foster siblings helped me settle into the reality of this unfamiliar space becoming my home until my eighteenth birthday. Having peers to guide me in those early weeks in the Ferguson home also helped me suppress my feelings of loss and loneliness when missing my mother and sister, wondering how they were doing, worrying if they were safe with my father or they were living someplace else without him. I also missed Cathy and Bill; I wished I could figure out a way to get their telephone number to call them, thinking it would be nice to hear a familiar voice.

In the early days of my arrival at the Fergusons', each of the kids would take the opportunity to give me their individual versions of the house rules:

1. On school days, the boys usually took their showers at night so we girls could have the bathroom in the morning. The eldest girl got to shower first because she had to be at school earlier that the others.
2. We could eat whatever was in the refrigerator across from the washing machine. The other refrigerator by the dining room table was off-limits; only Mom, Dad, and Marlene were allowed to use that refrigerator. We would get in trouble if we ate their food. Being teenagers, we would occasionally look in the Ferguson family refrigerator, which was stuffed with tasty foods like cheese slices, lunchmeat, fresh fruit, jams, milk, eggs, and bread—foods you would expect to see in both refrigerators but was not. Sometimes we would be bold enough to sneak a few slices of cheese, lunchmeat, or cooked leftovers, making sure we coordinated with one another to avoid taking a noticeable amount.
3. Our breakfast was always from the Hostess day-old bakery where Mom and Marlene go to shop every two weeks to buy honey buns, mini donuts, and fruit-filled Danishes, which were always in a Hostess box on top of the washing machine. Day-old baked goods were the only breakfast food made available to us; occasionally,

there was milk in our refrigerator to wash down these usually stale pastries. I ate so many honey buns for breakfast while living with the Fergusons, eventually getting so sick of them that I could not even look at one, much less eat one for the rest of my life.

The dinners Mom served us were usually something out of a can or box, including mac and cheese (not the good cheesy Kraft brand but a brand that had so little cheese, it tasted like plain cooked macaroni), usually served with canned peas or green beans, and inexpensive frozen TV dinners. We preferred the occasional Salisbury steak dinners over the soggy fried chicken dinners and Dinty Moore beef stew. Mom would make a point to tell us every time she bought Dinty Moore that we were getting a treat because it was "so expensive." "Served" is a misnomer because Mom would simply heat up whatever was for dinner and then call us into the kitchen to serve ourselves from the pot on the stove or to unwrap our TV dinners. Mom would usually sit at the table with us while we ate dinner, asking about our day. Mom was pleasant; she just was not generous.

When we would ask Mom if she would buy some different foods for us like hamburgers, fruits, lunchmeat to make sandwiches, eggs, or cereal with milk for breakfast, foods that were not boxed or frozen, she would say, "This is not a restaurant. Besides, I do not have time to cook meals for you, especially when all of you are in and out of the house at different times."

We said we could cook our own meals.

"No, no. It would be too much of a mess. You're fine eating what I make for you."

"We clean the kitchen after dinner now. What would be the difference if we cooked too?"

"I am not going to allow you to cook. End of subject."

4. We had to do our own laundry, but we couldn't use the washing machine. We had to go to the laundromat to wash our clothes. Mom would give us money for the washing machines and laundry soap. We girls usually combined our dirty clothes on weekends to go to the laundromat together to try to save some money to buy *beanos*, mini fried corn tortillas smeared with authentic refried beans that had been cooked with lard, sprinkled with cheese and hot sauce. Four *beanos* cost $1 at the Mexican drive-through conveniently located in the same shopping center as the laundromat.

5. Mom and Dad did not check to see if we did our homework. They trusted us to do our best in school, to get good grades to avoid negative consequences. When they got our report cards, which were sent directly to them, if you had bad grades, you lost your privileges.
6. We all had chores assigned to us that we had to get done before we could go anywhere on the weekend. Mom did not care who did what, so we took turns cleaning our bathroom and sweeping and mopping the kitchen and hallway. The boys had to mow the lawn on weekends, so the girls usually washed the dinner dishes. Then there were the kitchen windows; nobody liked cleaning the louvered windows, so we alternated turns every two weeks. We created a system of two per team to wash the windows together, one person swabbing each glass panel with hot soapy water, the other team member following behind to dry each pane of glass with used newspapers. Washing the louvered windows at the front of the house was by far the most tedious job—six louvered windows each with twelve individual glass panes.

We all grumbled about our chores, but we also knew once we got our work done, we were free to go wherever we wanted and to do whatever we wanted as long as we stayed out of trouble. Looking back, doing chores made us kids work together as a team with the same goal, finishing the tasks quickly so we could enjoy free time. Completing chores to earn privileges was a good lesson, giving me a good sense of accomplishment and teaching me the benefit of working together with others to achieve a mutual outcome.

Marlene liked to talk to the teenage brothers a lot. All of us could see that she had developed quite a fondness for the youngest brother, which he encouraged because he was a kind person, whereas the eldest brother was a big flirt but always looked out for us girls, keeping an eye on us like a big brother. Marlene was nice to all of us kids. I think she was lonely, never going anywhere but work, never having friends visit her, so it made sense to us that she liked hanging with the older kids, even though she was at least eleven years older than the eldest foster kid. Marlene began to share some useful information as she became more comfortable in her friendships with all of us.

One useful bit of information was that Mom received a monthly check for each of us foster kids. Each check was a couple of hundred dollars to pay for our food and clothing. This was news for most of us, who had no idea that foster parents received monthly paychecks to feed and clothe us. We had never thought about the financial aspect of living in a foster home, but it makes sense that the state would provide the necessary funds to feed and clothe us. Once we knew that Mom and Dad were receiving money to feed us, we began to wonder why the food we were provided was lacking in quality and variety, why Mom had not purchased new clothes for any of us, instead giving each of us a small allowance once a week. I do not recall the amount of the allowance, but I know it was not enough to buy clothes. I would have to save a month's worth of allowances to buy one, maybe two pieces of clothing at the White Front (1970s version of Walmart) department store.

Knowing that Mom was getting money to feed us made us kids feel resentment toward her for not keeping a steady supply of milk, lunchmeat, and foods that were not from the day-old or discount stores. We called the canned goods from the discount stores "dented discount foods." The older kids came up with the plan to call social services to complain about improper care, knowing there would not be any repercussions against us because the identity of the person who called had to remain anonymous to the foster parents. Social workers were supposed to make random, unannounced visits to licensed foster homes to ensure that the kids were being treated well, so we felt confident that Mom would not suspect that we had any involvement in a random visit from a social worker.

Mom and Marlene began to go away on weekends once or twice per month. I would learn later that Mom loved Las Vegas; she was using the money from social services to fund bimonthly trips to gamble, often taking Marlene with her for company. The bright side of Mom going to Las Vegas was that Dad interacted with us more, letting us eat whatever we wanted out of their refrigerator, allowing us to sit at the dinner table to eat with him, slipping each of us a few extra dollars to "buy yourself a treat." All of us enjoyed spending time with Dad. We looked forward to Mom taking her weekend trips to Las Vegas so we could have our quality time with him. We shared a secret bond with Dad that made each of us kids feel loved instead of feeling like commodities. Although we kids were frustrated with Mom for spending the money intended for our food and clothing on gambling, we appreciated the time we had with Dad, who was kind to all of us, and we enjoyed sitting together at the kitchen table like a family.

When I was at home, I would spend most of my time with Tammy, a sweet girl with an easy smile. She and I would walk to school together, meeting up for lunch most days, until she started ditching school and hanging out with a couple of her girlfriends who liked to hang out with a group of boys. Our time together at school lessened as I began to build friendships with other kids whom I met in my classes.

My interaction with the older kids was limited to home because they attended high school; even when they were home, they would focus on getting their homework done to get out of the house as quickly as possible to go hang with friends.

A couple of months after I had arrived, another girl moved into the Ferguson home. She was a couple of years older than me, abandoned by her parents shortly after they had arrived in the United States. This new girl had an easy disposition, always trying to make everyone laugh. She and I would become fast, close friends, spending most of our free time together, listening to music, dancing, and antagonizing the others until they would join us.

I would also learn some bad habits from my new foster sister, including sneaking out of the house late at night to go to the local pool hall to hang out with the owner, her "boyfriend," and sometimes other friends of his. I enjoyed the thrill of sneaking out of the house to go have fun shooting pool and dancing until the group of friends eventually became just me, my foster sister, her boyfriend, and one of his friends, whom they suggested "I be more friendly toward." At first, I did not understand what they meant. I thought I had been friendly to everyone. I would come to understand what "more friendly" meant when the friend tried to kiss me one night, suggesting that we "have fun together like your sister and her boyfriend." I emphatically said no and then yelled for my foster sister to come out of the office where she was with her boyfriend. I told her that I was going home with or without her.

Of course, she tried to laugh off what was going on, saying to me, "Everything's okay. We're just having fun."

I told her that I was not having fun and was going home.

She did leave with me, apologizing on the way home for leaving me alone. "I thought you were okay hanging out with that dude."

"I am okay hanging out with people. I am not okay being left alone with someone who thinks he can make out with me just because you are making out with your boyfriend. From now on, we do not leave each other alone with any guy."

Sneaking out to the pool hall with her became less fun as she spent more time with her boyfriend instead of playing pool, so I persuaded Tammy to sneak out with us a couple of times before we were busted by Marlene, who caught us sneaking back in through our bedroom window. I was almost glad that we got caught because I had become bored with playing pool and sneaking around in the dark.

The older kids naturally settled into the roles of being elder brothers and sisters to Tammy and me. The older girls would take Tammy and me to thrift stores or sales at White Front to help us buy the most clothes with our limited clothing stipend provided by the state, while the boys were our protectors.

I was comfortable living with this group of kids, each of us having suffered some trauma in our young lives that brought us together at this house to share the experience of making the best of our circumstances.

Eighth Grade

My first six months living with the Fergusons were uneventful as I eased into the eighth grade at Washington Junior High. School had always been my sanctuary, a place where I knew my father could not bother me, a place to make friends, a place to learn. Now that I was living in a safe environment, I was able to focus better on my schoolwork, earning myself a spot on the honor roll list at the end of my first semester of eighth grade.

When I was not at school, reading became a way to occupy my mind. Reading was a distraction from missing my mother, a respite from wondering if she would ever be able to take care of herself without my father, wondering when, if ever, she would come take me out of foster care, wondering if she knew where I lived.

I escaped my thoughts by reading. I read twenty books in my eighth-grade year, earning an achievement certificate in the Royal Order of Bookworms Club, along with a photo shot with my fellow bookworms for our school yearbook. A few stories stuck with me—*A Tree Grows in Brooklyn*, *To Kill a Mockingbird*, *Lord of the Flies*, and *Gone with the Wind*, all stories about people who had to endure setbacks, adversity, and griefs, yet they were able to move forward to overcome their circumstances. Reading these stories affected my young mind as I imagined myself overcoming the unfortunate circumstances set before me with the same determination as some of the characters in the books I read. Reading was my escape as well as a good discipline for me as I was subtly forming my study habits with some of the books being required reading toward my English class grade.

Photos of me in the chieftain yearbook are quite a contrast when I look at my frowning face in the honor roll group picture versus my smiling face in the bookworms picture. I wish I could recall the thoughts in my head of these contrasting moods reflected in my face on those days, especially my frowning face. I should have been smiling because I was wearing my new fake-rabbit-fur double-button coat gifted to me by one of my friends' elder brother. When he saw how much I liked the gray coat he had purchased for his sister, he gifted the same coat to me in white—"The two of you spend so much time together, you're like sisters. You might as well match each other."

I knew that going to school to learn as much as I could was important. I knew an education would be valuable in preparing me for getting a job in the future. I was always conscious of the fact that I would be on my own as soon as I turned eighteen. I needed to figure out what type of job I wanted while I was in high school because there were no guarantees that I would go to college.

Fortunately, making friends in school was easy for me, a quality about myself that I later recognized was a lifesaving attribute that began with the friendship I had with Cindy M. and her family. I think my smile was my icebreaker; a sincere smile is rarely rejected. The gift of an easy smile came from my mother; I vividly remember as a toddler staring up at my mother's face to see her bright red lip-sticked smile, which filled me with joy and love. My mother—who suffered pain, loss, sorrow, and abuse—never lost her brilliant smile, a gift from her soul.

I also had the confidence to talk to almost anyone, a trait honed from having to justify my every move to my drunk father, who had often challenged me to convince him why he should let me out of the house to be with my friends. Actually, there had been no convincing my father of anything; our conversations were more antagonistic, requiring me to stand my ground against him, helping me build my confidence as I held a strong position, arguing for myself. My father was trying to break me down by telling me how stupid I was, and I was trying to piss him off so I could point out that a thirteen-year-old had just made him lose control.

"Marie, I worry about you. You're too stupid to make decisions on your own, too stupid to take care of yourself."

"I am not stupid. If I were stupid, why do I get all Bs in school?"

Mockingly, my father responded, "Look at Marie, thinking she's smart because she gets Bs in seventh grade. Seventh grade doesn't mean shit! Seventh grade isn't going to teach you anything about the real world."

"If seventh grade doesn't mean shit, then why do you insist I go to school? Would it be better if I stayed at home, doing nothing like you do? All you do is get drunk, hit Mom, and argue with a thirteen-year-old."

I knew as the words came out of my mouth what was going to happen next. I braced myself. My father got up from where he was sitting to slap me across the face so hard, he knocked me off balance.

"Don't you ever take that tone of voice with me. I keep a fucking roof over your head and food in your stomach. Don't you ever disrespect me like that again."

Defending myself in almost every conversation I had with my father was my training ground for reading mood and intent. Surviving conversations with my father helped build my confidence to literally talk to anyone, which helped me make friends wherever I landed. My life motto after surviving my father became "What is the worst that can happen?" Talking to strangers, standing up for myself, and asking for a job were all made easier because the worst that could happen would be a simple "no" response.

Friendships

Eighth grade at Washington Junior High was where I met the two best friends who would be by my side through high school and beyond.

My first best friend was a pretty blonde, always smiling and flirting with the boys; actually, they were always flirting with her. I would spend a lot of time at her house during our eighth-grade year because the Fergusons did not allow us foster kids to bring friends into the Van Ruiten house; we could only hang out in the front yard if we brought friends over.

It was easy and relaxing to hang out with her at her house, where she lived with her single mother and younger brother. I used to think that her mom was a cool witch because she had an adult owl for a pet who calmly sat uncaged, one claw chained to a perch, following our every move with his rotating neck. I have no idea why I associated owls with sorcery, maybe because my friend's mom was always dressed in colorful flowing robes with large crystal necklaces hanging off her wrists and neck, seemingly with nothing to do but read and listen to music.

My friend and I would spend a lot of time together during our eighth-grade year, listening to music albums, mostly Chicago, dancing to "25 or 6 to 4" and "Make Me Smile," or talking about boys while listening to the Carpenters, Carole King or Al Green. I was often invited to stay and have dinner at their house, sometimes spending the night a couple of times a month so we could go to friends' house parties to dance or just hang out.

By the end of the school year, friends referred to us as the "Two Musketeers" because we were seemingly always together at school or at parties on the weekends. My friend liked the attention we were getting from the boys, and there always seemed to be a boy who was interested in her. I was quickly tired of telling boys who assumed that I was down for making out because "your friend does" that I did not make out. I admired my friend for going after what she wanted, which, at the time, seemed to be the attention of boys and wanting a steady boyfriend, but I was more interested in going to parties to dance, to hang with girls and boys who also liked to dance. Dancing was my happy place.

My decision to get a job and take a break from parties turned out to be good instinct based on entries in my eighth-grade yearbook: "You're a cool girl... Good luck with the boys," "To a cool girl, have fun this summer... Good luck with the boys," "Been fun knowing you. You are a sweet girl. I hope to see you next year. Good luck with the boys this summer." It makes me laugh when I read these entries because I must have been oblivious. I always felt that the boys were interested in my friend. I was not interested in having a steady boyfriend, other than hanging with them as friends, until my sophomore year in high school, when I would ask Jon to be my date for the Sadie Hawkins dance.

When summer arrived, I told my friend that I was going to focus on getting a job because I wanted to earn money to buy clothes for myself. Mom only gave us $50 to buy clothes for the entire school year, which was not much when you considered that we had to buy shoes and all of our clothing, even underwear.

So it came to be that both of us got summer jobs at different fast-food restaurants, lessening our time together during my first summer with the

Fergusons. My job was at a falafel drive-through where I learned to grind chickpeas to form into flat round disks that could be breaded and fried or pickled to put into pita bread with yogurt, tomatoes, and lettuce. I was glad that I had a job, but I was already planning to find a different job as soon as possible because I did not like my hair and clothes smelling like fried food at the end of every shift.

Over the summer, I explored my friendship with another girl I had met at school, Roxanne. She was chill and funny and shared my love for all things outdoors. Roxanne and I became friends when we were assigned to be tennis partners in our physical education class. We were naturally athletic but had more fun laughing at ourselves and goofing on the courts to make others laugh, including our PE teacher, Ms. Hays, who would often say to me, "Keep smiling, Joannes. Your personality shines through your smile"—confirmation from an adult authority that I absorbed as encouragement.

Roxanne lived with her grandmother, who allowed her to have a lot of freedom to make her own decisions as long as she continued to do well in school. I do not recall Roxanne discussing her parents. At the time, I didn't give much thought to her living conditions. I was content enjoying our friendship, her calm demeanor and dry sense of humor, all traits that made hanging with her easy and fun. Life slowed down when Roxanne and I were together. I felt like I was developing a strong sense of who I was as the end of my eighth-grade school year ended. Granted, I was only going to be fourteen years old in June, yet I sensed that good things were going to happen for me. I probably felt this way because Roxanne and I talked a lot about getting jobs, finishing school, and living on our own. We believed that anything was possible for us.

Roxanne and I loved going to the beach so much so that we spent most of our summer with our thumbs stuck out on Bellflower Boulevard, wearing bikini bathing suits with shorts covering our bottoms, hitchhiking for rides to Huntington Beach or Seal Beach, a straight shot down Bellflower Boulevard to the sand.

Looking back, I am surprised that we made it to ninth grade. The 1970s were prolific years for serial killers, and California seemed to have its fair share: the Golden State Killer, the I-5 Strangler, the Hillside Strangler, and the Dating Game Killer, who prowled our favorite spot in Huntington Beach, photographing young girls, sadly abducting one of his victims from our favorite spot, Sunset Beach. We were barely teenagers getting into cars with complete strangers, with our only plan of escape if something were to go wrong being "jump out of the car, moving or not, and run." We were fearless together and also very lucky.

Roxanne and I became so confident in our hitchhiking skills that we did not hesitate to say yes when one of my foster brothers asked us if we wanted to join him and one of his buddies to hitchhike from Bellflower to the Colorado River, a three-hundred-mile trip, give or take a few miles, on a summer holiday weekend before school started. I trusted my foster brother. My relationships with all of the elder siblings had developed into mutual respect, with me often looking to them for advice.

The brothers would often say to us girls in their thick Yugoslavian accents, "Think of us as your Yugoslavian brothers, your protectors, your advisors. Come to us for anything." They were fun and funny, guys who embraced the roles of being big brothers.

Our plan was for me to ask Mom if I could spend the weekend with Roxanne and her family, who were going to camp at the Colorado River. Roxanne told her grandmother that she was going to the river with a few friends whose parents were driving us to the river in a camping van. Both of us were happy when we got permission to go, yet we also felt guilty for lying because we appreciated that our guardians trusted us enough to say yes to our requests. It was our nature to do what we were told, so we were feeling pretty guilty the days before our planned trip, but we were also filled with excitement to begin the journey.

I arrived at Roxanne's house early in the morning the day we were to leave for the Colorado River. Then we went to meet my foster brother and his friend in our neighborhood White Front department store parking lot, where our journey would begin with a group of his friends who would be driving us to a truck stop in Indio, almost halfway to Lake Havasu, where we would then have to hitch a ride the rest of the way. We had one rule: "Do not split up." If we had to ride in separate vehicles because of space, we agreed that we would do so as one boy and one girl.

We arrived at the Indio truck stop midday, a good time because there were lots of cars, vans, and trucks at this large facility, which, to us, meant we had a good chance of getting a ride quickly. Roxanne and I went inside the store to go to the restroom and buy some sodas and snacks, while the guys stayed outside to scope out our next ride. By the time Roxanne and I came out of the store, my foster brother had secured rides to Havasu with a group of people who had two vehicles with room for the four of us.

Of course, the one rule we had agreed upon had to change because the two vehicles were different families traveling together who did not want to split up their groups just so the four of us could stay together. We were anxious to get to the river; it was daylight, and one group had women, so we felt comfortable enough to go in separate vehicles. We felt so comfortable that we broke our one rule. Roxanne and I rode together in a van with two guys and two girls, while the guys rode in the back of a pickup truck with the other guys in the group.

I'm not going to lie—Roxanne and I were a little nervous being in the back of a panel van with only the windshield and two port windows to look outside, trying to keep our eyes on the truck that the guys were in. Knowing they had the license number of the van Roxanne and I were in and we had the license number of the truck they were in made the situation slightly less scary; however, this was the summer of 1971. Before cell phones, we were depending on the kindness of strangers.

Fortunately for us, our driving hosts were kind, delivering the four of us safely to our designated meeting spot safe and sound, where we met up with the rest of our friends, who had set up an encampment of tents, including one for Roxanne and me to share with my foster brother and his travel buddy. We enjoyed a couple of fun days swimming and tubing in the river. Like most vacations, time passed quickly, and before we knew it, we were heading back to Bellflower, the four of us in one truck courtesy of new friends who showed up at the river mid-weekend. Roxanne and I were happy; we did not have the stress of worrying about getting home safely.

Looking back on this adventurous and irresponsible trip is a cause for reflection on the amount of freedom Mom and Dad allowed their charges to enjoy. I wonder, was allowing us so much freedom a way for us to learn to make our own decisions, right or wrong, a test to see how we would handle the responsibility? A training ground for adulthood? Or were the Fergusons simply indifferent about what we did as long as they were not being bothered by our behaviors? Whatever their intent, I appreciated living in a peaceful, safe home with adults I knew would not harm me and would most likely provide guidance if I asked. I appreciated the simplicity of having freedom, being young and unaware of the consequences that might otherwise make me hesitate before venturing forward toward outcomes unknown.

I believed that telling us we had to get jobs to earn spending money to buy clothes and personal items was Mom Ferguson's way of exposing us to budgeting money so we would be somewhat prepared when we aged out of foster care. I wanted to believe that Mom genuinely cared about us and wasn't simply providing the basic care for the reward of a monthly check for each foster kid housed on Van Ruiten.

Social services had not provided any type of counsel to me about the steps I needed to take to successfully mature out of foster care. I learned from the older foster kids that I would have to work to support myself. They told me to start thinking about what kind of job I wanted to do so I could take classes or get jobs that would prepare me for working when I turned eighteen. I already knew that I wanted to be a secretary or a nurse. My plan was to take typing and shorthand classes in high school, thinking that both skills would be useful for either occupation.

High School = Opportunity

A note was delivered to me during my second period class on my first day of ninth grade at Bellflower High School (BHS). I was immediately worried, thinking something bad must have happened to require that I be pulled from class on my first day of high school. I opened the note with much apprehension: "Mr. Sienknecht would like to see you in his office at lunch break today." Mr. Sienknecht was the counselor for the class of 1975, the class I would graduate with. I put the note inside my notebook, trying not to think about it until lunch break.

As soon as I walked into Mr. Sienknecht's office, he stood up from his chair to step out from behind his desk with a big smile on his face to greet me by taking my hand in his, looking directly at me with his warm, kind eyes. "You have to be Joannes."

"Yes, I am," I said nervously.

"Here, sit. Sit here in front of the desk. I will sit in this chair next to you so we can talk."

After we had both settled into our chairs, Mr. Sienknecht said, "You must be wondering why I called you into my office on your first day of high school."

"Yes. I was a little worried, thinking I can't be in any trouble. I just started school here today."

My comment made him chuckle. I smiled at him, enjoying our moment of connection.

"You are correct. You are not in any trouble. In fact, I was reviewing your grades from Washington Junior High. I see you are a smart young lady."

"Thank you," I said. "I like school."

"Good, good. We counselors like to hear our students say they like school. It usually makes our job easier," he said with a smile. "I like to meet all of my kids when they start their school year, especially kids from the Fergusons' home. Mrs. Ferguson always gives me a call to let me know when she has kids coming to school here. I want you to know I am here for you should you need anything. I mean it. Anything. My job is to help you become the best you, to help you find opportunities to become whatever you want to be."

Mr. Sienknecht was my second guide. Yes, he was a guidance counselor, but I felt then and now that he went beyond his job title by taking the time to make an emotional connection with me, often checking in with me to ask how I was doing, asking if I needed anything. I was mesmerized by his contagious energy and enthusiasm, looking into his warm, kind eyes, absorbing the powerful words he had just delivered to me: *"to help you become the best you, to help you become whatever you want to be."*

This was the first time in my life that an adult had told me I could become anything I wanted to be, the first time an adult told me they would be there to help me achieve my goals. I believed Mr. Sienknecht because I sensed that he believed in me. I felt he was going to be a person who would help guide me through high school, showing me the path toward opportunities to improve my circumstances. He helped me believe in myself.

Mr. Sienknecht walked behind his desk to retrieve two sandwiches wrapped in wax paper. "I made cheese sandwiches for us, knowing I would be pulling you away from your lunch break. Would you like potato chips or an apple with your sandwich?"

"I would like the apple, please."

"How about a drink? Would you like a soda or water?"

"Soda, please."

"Okay. Now let's enjoy our lunch together while you tell me about the classes you are enrolled in. I want to know what you have planned for your freshman year."

I told him that my first period class was typing because I wanted to be a secretary or a nurse when I graduated from high school and I thought

I would need to know how to type for either job. Then there were the required classes: English, algebra, social sciences, and PE.

Mr. Sienknecht liked my thought process. "Fantastic! You have a nice variety of subjects. You will do well."

He suggested that I consider taking a journalism or writing class in the second semester to expand my vocabulary. I also chose French for one of my elective classes with Staci because we wanted to travel to France together when we graduated from high school. My maternal grandparents came to the United States from France; Staci's paternal grandparents were also from France. I took French class every quarter of my freshman year. Staci and I even joined the French Club together to learn more about the country and practice speaking with our classmates. Sadly, I did not retain any of the language.

I was excited to settle into high school. I had great optimism for my future. I knew that a good education was my path to successfully age out of foster care, whether I continued onto college or started a career. I was confident that my future lay in my hands if I worked to achieve good grades. Having my two best friends with me made my transition from junior high to high school easier because I was able to confide in them, share classes with them, and make many new friends together during our time at BHS.

I took the advice of my eldest foster sister, letting her introduce me to Mr. McDowell, the journalism teacher and advisor for the *Blade*, our school newspaper, where she was currently the VariTypist. (The VariTyper was basically a typewriter that would automatically rewind the carriage at the end of each line, used to create forms; it is now in the National Museum of American History.) This introduction would prove beneficial for me because she taught me how to operate the VariTyper, preparing me to take her place on the *Blade* staff in my sophomore year. In addition to typing, working on the school newspaper gave me the opportunity to hone my spelling and vocabulary skills while collaborating with others and meeting deadlines.

This first year of high school passed quickly. Making new friends, enjoying my classes, doing homework with my foster sibs—I was happily settled into a safe life.

The eldest of the foster brothers had already moved out by this time after graduating high school the previous year to go work at his father's car wash, leaving his younger brother to complete his senior year. He returned to the Van Ruiten house most Saturday mornings to pick his brother up and take him to Long Beach to work weekends for their father.

Freshman year ended eleven days before my fifteenth birthday, just in time for Roxanne and me to return to our summer routine of weekend jaunts to the beaches, celebrating my birthday with a few friends, cooking hot dogs and marshmallows on sticks over the beach firepit.

Roxanne and I decided that we should give up hitchhiking to the beach. We were finally sensing the dangers of getting into cars with strangers. We chose to make the fourteen-mile trip by bus to Seal Beach instead of hitchhiking, thinking it was faster and definitely safer. Sometimes the guys would drop us off at Seal Beach before continuing their drive to work at the car wash. I had also become pretty good friends with our next-door neighbor, who would offer to drop us off at a bus stop on his way to work, which was halfway to the beach, giving us more time on the sand, less time on the bus.

I was enjoying my new life so much that I forgot to miss my mother and sister. I had not heard from my mother—no letters, no telephone calls. Maybe it was my self-centered teenage ego. Maybe I loved my new life so much that it made it easier for me to not be sad about missing my mother and sister. Whatever the reason, I chose to thrive in foster care and not worry about my mother; she could find out where I was if she wanted to find me. I decided that I was not going to hold onto the hope of living with my mother. I did not want to be disappointed again.

New Family Member

The summer also brought a new resident to Van Ruiten. Mom and Dad's twenty-five-year-old son Jim had returned home from Vietnam, completing his two years of service with the army. Mom and Dad moved out of their bedroom to give their room to their son, moving themselves into Dad's den. I found it strange that no attempt was made to introduce Jim to any of us foster kids. I brushed it off as just another example of the separation of the Ferguson family from us foster kids, keeping us at a distance so we never quite felt like we were actually part of their family.

A few weeks would pass before any of us would actually meet Jim, even though he was across the hall, one door down from our room. We were beginning to think that he really wasn't in the house or that he only left his room when none of us were around.

Our first impression of Jim was not a good one. We thought that he was mean and rude to his father. Dad would knock on Jim's door every morning, around 7:00 a.m., to tell him it was time to get ready for work. Jim never got up on the first knock. Dad would walk back to the kitchen table to finish eating his morning cheese sandwich, with his pot of dark tea steeping, waiting for him to transfer the hot black liquid into his work thermos that he took with him every workday.

Dad's second attempt to rouse Jim out of bed often involved yelling and mild swearing. "Get your arse out of bed! I am leaving at 8:00 a.m. You better be in my truck, or I will leave without you, and you damn well know you will not be paid for the day."

It was a little unsettling to hear Dad yell with anger because he had always been kind to us kids. He always had a smile for us and never raised his voice when talking to us. Of course, we had not given Dad any reason to raise his voice. We had too much respect for him.

Jim would always yell back a few obscenities, ending in "leave me alone." He never got up on Dad's first request. This interaction occurred while we kids were getting ready for school, so we could see and hear Dad as well as hear Jim's obscene, angry replies, often followed by a boot being thrown at Dad, sometimes barely missing his head. I guess Jim did not want to get up until all of us kids had left for school because we always had to leave before 8:00 a.m. to get to our first class on time. We girls thought that Jim was a total jerk. We did not like him being mean to Dad. We wished Dad would just leave for work without Jim, but we knew Dad needed the help.

My foster brother was the first of us kids to meet Jim when he returned home late from work one night and saw Jim sitting in the garage, playing his guitar, taking the opportunity to spend some time getting to know Jim, asking him how he was adjusting to being back in the States. Jim told him he was having a hard time adjusting to a regular schedule and being back home, living with his parents.

Jim said that his intention was to be on his own when he returned home from the army, that he had planned to be able to live on his own with the money he sent home every month to his mother to save for him, but instead of putting the money in the bank for Jim, his mother spent all of his savings on her trips to Las Vegas. We kids were not surprised when we heard the story about Mom gambling away her son's savings; we already knew she was obsessed with spending money in Las Vegas.

Now Jim's crankiness about getting up for work made a little more sense. Living in his parents' house, shared with foster kids, was probably not how he had envisioned his life when he returned home. Still, we girls thought Jim should be nicer to Dad, who was working his butt off for all of us.

On most nights, the two guys would hang out in the garage, talking, smoking, my foster brother trying to learn how to play the guitar with Jim's help. Soon, the rest of us kids would gather in the garage to listen to them practice, ranking on his rusty guitar skills just to get a few good laughs. We did not get to pick on our brother too long before his beginning skill level improved. He learned how to play the guitar quickly and was soon jamming with Jim and the other guys from the neighborhood who had formed a small band, often practicing in our garage a few nights a week, with weekend nights evolving into a mini neighborhood concert.

Even Marlene, whom we did not see very often because she was busy working most nights at the local Kmart, would join us kids in the garage to listen to the guy's practice, with all of us eventually moving into the front yard, acting like we were at a live concert, dancing and having fun. For a brief time, the Fergusons' house was the place to hang out on hot summer nights as long as we stayed out of the house. Mom never allowed us to bring friends into the house.

By the end of summer, I had a crush on Jim. I was drawn to his musical talent—no surprise since I was always drawn to music. I was probably more enamored with the fact that Jim played his guitar well. He was a good musician, feeding my love of music, allowing me to manifest the few good memories of dancing with my mother as a child to her favorite songs or listening to music together as a family when our family life was normal and peaceful. Music had always been a comforting source for me to go to when I needed to hear a song to help me through pain, to release my tears, or a song that would instantly make me want to dance, filling me with joy. Music was also the catalyst to making friends in high school, building friendships at the school dances, bonding over our shared love of music and dancing.

I found Jim's quiet, confident demeanor soothing, unlike my father or any of his male friends, whose behavior was often a loud and erratic presence in our house, with the exception of Guide One, who also had a calm, kind, inviting presence. I felt a connection building between Jim and me, especially when he would smile at me, looking at me with his dark brown eyes, discreetly holding my gaze, making me feel like I was the only person he was looking at, even when there were other people around us. No words had to be exchanged. I felt an unspoken connection forming between us, a sense of excitement building in me, making me want to find ways to spend more time with Jim.

One evening Jim asked me to come sit next to him on the bench in the garage so he could show me how to play the guitar. My foster brother who was also practicing encouraged me to give the guitar a try.

"You can be the only girl in our man band," he said.

I teased him, replying, "Man band? I do not see any men in this garage."

We laughed at each other. We were always ragging on each other, like any big brother and younger sister would do.

I was too self-conscious about messing up and too nervous to concentrate while sitting so close to Jim, so after several minutes of Jim trying to show me the chords, I got up and moved to the other side of the garage, telling Jim I would rather listen to him play, unless he wanted to teach me how to play the drums because drums were the only instrument I was interested in learning. Jim told me that one of his friends could teach me how to play the drums, but I would have to buy a set of drums to practice on.

I said, "That's not going to happen anytime soon in my life, unless you know how I can get a set without money."

On most evenings, after doing homework and eating dinner, I would go to the garage to listen to the guys practice playing their guitars. Soon, I was the only girl in the house interested in hanging out to listen to them play. My foster sisters had gotten bored several weeks before, preferring to walk to the nearby shopping center or stay in the house to watch television. They would often tease me about my crush on our foster brother, which I was okay with; having their suspicion directed at him meant that I was doing a good job hiding my affection for Jim.

I had always been close to the youngest of the brothers; he had even tried to kiss me once when he was slightly inebriated, but I brushed him off, telling him that it would be weird to kiss my brother. I never had romantic feelings for him; in my heart, he had always been a big brother to me, someone I could easily talk to, someone I knew had my back. I think I may have embarrassed him after I rejected his kiss because his playful attitude with me changed quickly afterward. He slowly distanced himself from me. Eventually, he even stopped hanging out with Jim if I was in the garage. He was smart; I am sure he could probably see the connection building between Jim and me, and it hurt him. It made me sad, knowing his feelings were hurt, even sadder when he began to spend less time in the garage playing his guitar. Soon, he stopped showing up at all.

I regret that my affection for Jim distracted me from my friendship with my foster brother because I lost my opportunity to say to him, "You are my brother. I will always have love for you in my heart." Before I knew it, he had aged out of the foster care system, leaving to live and work with his father. So it came to be that there were times when only Jim and I were together in the garage.

One evening Jim moved over to sit closer to me, saying, "It looks like it's just you and me now."

Then he leaned over and kissed me on the lips. I was not surprised by his kiss; nor did I say anything when the kiss ended. I had secretly been wondering what it would be like to be kissed by Jim, who leaned in close to my ear—"Did you like my kiss?"

I replied nervously, "Yes, I did."

Then he cupped my face in his hands to kiss me again, longer this time. I felt a warm surge run through my body and between my legs. This was a new sensation for me that I wanted to explore.

Sophomore Year

Knowing that I had to make money for clothes and spending kept me motivated to find jobs. In my sophomore year, Mr. Sienknecht facilitated a job for me through a school–work program that allowed me to work a few days a week after school in the attendance office. I was paid minimum wage, which was about $2/hour in 1973. I was excited to have a job for the money and the opportunity to learn more office skills to prepare me for becoming a secretary, my dream job at the time.

I was nervous and excited when Mr. Sienknecht walked me from his office to the attendance office on a Monday after school to meet the two attendance clerks, Mrs. Hodge and Mrs. Garrison, who were in charge of the department and would be my supervisors. Both ladies greeted me with smiles on their faces, taking my hand in theirs to introduce themselves, welcoming me to my new job. I liked the sound of "my new job."

My clerk duties included filing, lots of filing of attendance cards and absentee notes from parents, along with the occasional opportunity to answer the telephones if Mrs. Hodge and Mrs. Garrison were busy helping students or teachers at the counter. More importantly, I learned the intangible skills of professionalism by watching my two supervisors communicate with people in a calm and friendly yet firm manner when sassy students came in to protest their attendance record or when speaking with their boss, the school principal. These two ladies were my first examples of women working, and being in charge in their field, they were excellent role models, showing me by example how to efficiently organize the various work tasks: typing, filing, and communicating with others in person or on the telephone.

I enjoyed my afterschool job. I did not mind working with just adults as some of my friends would suggest, "Don't you find it boring, working in an office where all the people are old enough to be your parents? What do you talk about?" I rarely thought about the age of people; to me, connecting with people of any age was an adventure as long as they were kind and caring. I especially enjoyed learning whatever I could from people who were genuinely interested in helping me achieve whatever goal I had set for myself. I appreciated healthy interactions with adults, something I did not have the first twelve years of my life.

An added benefit of working in the attendance office was having the school counselors walk by on the way to their offices, allowing Mr. Sienknecht the opportunity to stop to check in with me to ask me how I was doing, reminding me that his office door was always open should I need anything. His parting words were always "Imagine getting paid to work with wonderful kids like you." I cherish his handwritten note of this sentiment in my sophomore yearbook next to his picture.

My sophomore year was a time of self-discovery. Enough time had passed to wash away the fear that my father might somehow figure out a way to regain custody of me. Instead of hoping my mother was going to show up to take me to live with her, I decided to trust the care I had living in a foster home with kind people, enjoy my foster siblings, and put my focus toward my education to graduate high school.

This period of self-discovery gave me a strong sense of personal well-being. Every new friend I made, each good grade I achieved, every extracurricular school activity I participated in, and every job I got helped build my confidence and strengthen my desire to become better than the example of the life I had lived with my parents. I knew I had the ability to rise above my circumstances to build a better life for myself.

I think I was also motivated to achieve successes to be able to someday say to my father, "You did not break me. I am not stupid. I am not an idiot. I have become a strong, productive person in spite of you, not because of you."

School Dances, Friendships, Boys

I had a lot of fun in my sophomore year, making lots of new friends, working on the *Blade* staff, working after school, and going to most of the school dances with my girlfriends. All of us loved to dance, often walking onto the dance floor to dance with our friends in a group until a boy was brave enough to approach our group to ask us to dance. At one of the dances, a boy entered our circle of girls to dance with us. His name was John.

John and I were enthusiastic dancers who fit well together on the dance floor with our similar dance styles, which is to say the both of us had great rhythm and loved dancing to anything—funk, Motown, or disco—easily getting our groove on and often becoming the focus of dance circles at most of the school dances. We always encouraged others to dance with us, making us the go-to dancers for getting the fun started. John and I became good friends because of our love of dancing. We accidentally became the "life of the school dances" for the balance of the school year, enjoying every minute of recognition we received from our classmates and upper classmates.

After high school, John danced his way onto American Bandstand, becoming one of the AB dancers, winning the 1976 dance contest with his partner, Linda. I wish I had kept dancing with John. I would have liked to have auditioned to become a dancer on American Bandstand, but I would choose a different path. Dancing still brings me great joy.

It was through John that I met a cute, tall, somewhat quiet boy with a warm smile who played on the junior BHS basketball team, Jon (Jon and John were very popular names at BHS). Jon was my first high school crush. It was Jon's friendly smile that made me want to get to know him better, so I got up the nerve to ask him to the Sadie Hawkins dance, even though his dance style was more swaying in one spot than dancing.

My first date with Jon was a double date with my friend and her boyfriend, Brian, who was a senior and also a basketball player. Lucky for us, Brian had a car to chauffer us to Sam's Seafood in Seal Beach for our dinner before returning to BHS for the 7:00 p.m. dance kickoff. The date started off well as the guys got to know each other better, talking basketball. They both played on our school teams. This helped Jon relax a bit; he seemed really nervous. Brian was a jokester, making all of us laugh. By the time we had arrived at the restaurant, Jon was laughing and being more talkative throughout dinner. I accidentally made everyone laugh when I made a faux pas, ordering "lobster Labrador" instead of lobster Thermidor. I guess I was a little nervous, being on my first date. My friends razzed me for the rest of the night, asking me if I enjoyed the lobster Labrador.

I did not mind my friends teasing me because the humor put Jon at ease, so by the time we got to the dance, he was relaxed enough to walk into the gym, holding my hand to lead me onto the dance floor for the one dance, the only dance that Jon and I would have together that night because we arrived at the dance ninety minutes late because of the super slow service at the restaurant. Rookie mistake: never go to the same restaurant that half the other schools chose to have dinner at on Sadie Hawkins night. Jon's gesture, swaying in one spot on the dance floor, is one of my fondest high school memories because he knew how much I was looking forward to dancing that night; even though it was just one dance, it was memorable. Jon was my first and last true boyfriend in high school because I would soon be in love with someone else.

SECRETS

As the middle of my sophomore year approached, I was content, enjoying everything about living with the Fergusons. I no longer thought of myself as a foster kid living in a foster home. Van Ruiten Street was simply home.

I also had a big secret that made living on Van Ruiten Street even more exciting and also a bit stressful. My relationship with Jim had progressed beyond just friendship. Spending time together had moved from hanging out in the garage to outings away from the house, lunch in the park, and drives to the beach. Physical attraction for each other was building between us, evolving into clandestine meetings inside the camper shell on Jim's truck.

Mom and Dad usually retreated to their living area in the back of the house after dinnertime, allowing us kids to do pretty much anything we wanted to do. By now, I had been living in the Ferguson home for two years. During that time, I had given them no reason to not trust me. I felt slightly guilty when I would lie to Mom about going to a friend's house when I was actually going to a designated meeting spot to meet Jim.

I felt safe and loved when I was with Jim. He listened to me intently when I would talk about what I was doing at school, the classes I was taking, my friends, my journey to foster care, my family. Being listened to and feeling safe made me happy. Of course, like most teenage girls, I was content to tell Jim almost everything about myself, pressing him for little information about his time served in the army. When I did ask Jim questions about his army duty in Vietnam, he would say there wasn't much to tell, only telling me a few stories about his army buddies and the good times they had hanging out together, unwinding over the card game Mao, a favorite pastime, along with smoking lots of cigarettes.

One night, when a bunch of us were hanging out in the garage, I noticed Jim showing some of his friends a couple of guns he had removed from a case. I overheard Jim tell them that he had learned a lot about guns during his Vietnam tour, where he was trained to be a marksman. I took this opportunity to walk over to join their conversation.

"Hey, guys. I would like to hear about Jim's experience as a marksman. Is being a marksman different from the other soldiers who are also trained to shoot guns?"

Jim replied, "Yes, marksmen have specific targets."

"What do you mean when you say 'specific targets'? What did you shoot at?"

Jim simply replied, "Let's change the subject. I don't want to talk about what we were trained to shoot. I'm just showing off my gun collection."

I was taken aback by Jim's demeanor when he was asked too many questions about what he did while serving in the army. He would often become agitated, even withdrawn on those occasions when we would probe him about his time served in Vietnam. He was almost brusque before going quiet or changing the subject.

Of course, I had no true sense of what soldiers truly endured while serving in any war, much less the first major war lost abroad in American history. I was an ill-informed teenager, mindlessly sewing peace signs onto my jeans and tank tops, thinking I was making a statement against the war with no consideration for the soldiers who were fighting and dying in a conflict most Americans thought we should not be in. Soldiers returning home from the Vietnam War did not return to "welcome home" parades like soldiers in past wars. Instead, they were ignored or questioned by angry citizens who wanted to know why they had participated in a war that many U.S. citizens felt we should not have participated in.

I would wonder if Jim suffered from survivor's guilt like so many soldiers who made it home alive and intact when others did not, feeling deep regret for making it home alive unlike the 58,220 soldiers who died during the Vietnam War.[5] I came to understand why Jim did not want to talk about the time he had served in Vietnam. I made a mental note to never ask Jim about his duty in Vietnam unless he chose to talk to me about it.

Date Nights

Jim and I started venturing away from home together, mostly on weekend nights to the local drive-in movie theater, a great venue to hang out, enjoying a movie in the company of each other. Drive-ins were dark, making it unlikely that we would run into anyone we knew. Plus, we had privacy in the back of Jim's pickup truck with the attached camper shell, where he kept most of his work tools locked up. We would choose a parking space that Jim could easily back his truck into, a space away from other moviegoers to give us privacy while sitting on the tailgate, watching the movie.

More times than not, our intentions to watch the movie were hindered by the electricity building between us, turning movie night into make-out night. On one of our date nights, we decided to close the tailgate and crawl into the sleeping bags inside the camper when it got too chilly to continue sitting outside on the open tailgate. We crawled into two sleeping bags we had zipped together, propping ourselves up against the toolboxes, using

---

5   U.S. National Archives.

them as a headrest to be able to see the movie through the back camper shell opening. I think both of us knew we were moving inside the camper shell to have more privacy to move into our next step of sexual intimacy. In that, moment getting warm was a secondary need.

I snuggled in close to Jim's body to get warm inside our shared cocoon, kissing his neck, hoping he wanted to touch me.

Jim laughed. "I thought you wanted to finish watching the movie."

I asked, "Do you?"

"It depends. I will do whatever you are in the mood to do."

Nervously, I told Jim I was ready for the next step. "I want to do more than just kissing and touching with you. I want you to be my first."

"I would love to be the first to make love to you, but I want you to be sure this is what you want. Having intercourse for the first time is a big deal."

"I know this is a big decision. I also know it is my decision, and I choose you."

Jim pulled me in closer. "Okay. We will take it slow. You tell me if you ever feel uncomfortable as I guide you through what I hope you will think is a pleasurable experience."

I wanted my first time to be a big deal with the right person. I felt that Jim was that person. I needed him to be the one to show me what consensual intercourse was supposed to feel like. I wanted our lovemaking to erase the forced sexual assault memories stored in my head and my body. I was ready and willing to let Jim guide me through this experience in the back of his truck under a camper shell at a drive-in movie.

Nervously, I whispered, "Show me. Show me how much you love me."

Jim kissed me gently, saying, "Let's take off all of our clothes. I want to look at your naked body."

He reached to help me pull off my jeans and blouse. He reached to remove my panties.

As I was undoing my bra, I stopped him, saying, "You have to take off your clothes before I am completely naked. I want to see your body too."

Jim removed all of his clothes at warp speed, which made me laugh (relieving some of my nervousness from feeling so vulnerable in my nakedness) because he did it in a comical manner, exclaiming, "I'm ready!"

He gently pulled my body into his, kissing my neck and my breasts as he removed my panties. "Are you okay?" he asked.

"Yes. I like feeling your breath and lips on my body. Don't stop."

Jim slowly kissed my breasts, moving down my stomach to my crotch, kissing me where I had never been kissed before. I was enraptured. Jim quickly put a condom on (something I had not even considered in the heat of the moment—stupid!). Then he moved up to lie on top of me, inserting himself inside of me.

"Are you okay? Let me know if I'm hurting you."

It did hurt when Jim entered my body, but I wanted him to be rewarded for taking the time to satisfy me first. I relaxed, trying to enjoy the movement of our bodies together in unison until Jim reached completion. I felt his body exhale as he rolled off to the side of me. We lay together in silence, looking out at the stars in the sky. I felt safe. I felt loved.

Our trips to the drive-in became more about spending time together to have sex, often resulting in me barely making my 10:00 p.m. weekend curfew. As safe as I felt with Jim, I could not bring myself to tell him I had been raped by my father. I still felt that I was flawed because my body had been used for such a painful, ugly act. I knew Jim loved me, yet I could not shake the thought that he would somehow think less of me. I would not risk losing his love, his respect for me by telling him about the assault. I thought he might see me in a different way. I thought he would think I was damaged.

What I did not realize at the time was that *I* thought I was damaged. *I* was deflecting my thoughts about myself, even though Jim was gentle and attentive to my needs. I could not allow myself to fully enjoy the physical act of having intercourse. My enjoyment during intercourse was the emotional connection between Jim and me. The excitement and crescendo to conclusion that he achieved satisfied me. I felt good because he felt good.

I was hit with a reality check several weeks after Jim and I had started having intercourse when he made me acutely aware of what would happen if anyone found out about our relationship: "We will have to stop seeing each other if you tell anyone about us. No one, not even your best friends, can know we are having sex." Jim also stated on many occasions, "If you get pregnant, we are done . . . We're over."

Of course, I understood the importance of birth control. We had already decided on the pullout and rhythm methods. It was Jim's edicts delivered in a somewhat harsh manner that made me feel he was being selfish by putting most of the responsibility on me to avoid getting pregnant. He had convinced me that the "pulling out" birth control method was the best method for both of our enjoyment as long as I was diligent with tracking my periods. I finally lost my patience listening to him admonish me.

"Why don't you wear condoms if you are so concerned about me getting pregnant?" I asked.

He replied, "Condoms are not comfortable, and they reduce some of the pleasurable sensation. Plus, the withdrawal method is just as safe for birth control as wearing a condom."

I would challenge Jim's logic a couple of times, mostly because I was not convinced that the withdrawal method was as safe as using a condom. While pulling out is not as safe as using a condom, it is statistically 96 percent safe with accurate timing. I acquiesced because I was too afraid to take birth control pills, knowing they were the cause of my mother's stroke.

When I reflect on the number of times Jim and I met to have sex while we were living on Van Ruiten, I am struck by how selfish our actions were. If social services found out I was having sex with Jim, they would definitely have removed me from the house, most likely stripped the Fergusons of their foster care license, requiring that my foster siblings be placed elsewhere too.

I am still incredulous at the idea of Jim not taking full responsibility for birth control, unless he was unaware of the statutory rape laws. I prefer to think he was intelligent enough to know about the consequences but chose to ignore them because he was in love with me. However, he was in a precarious situation, having sexual intercourse with a minor. If anyone found out about our relationship, he would be arrested for statutory rape and most likely be sentenced to a jail term since he was ten years older than me. Our passion for each other blinded us from the consequences we could all suffer if anyone found out about our relationship.

As we spent more time together, we were made aware of suspicions among the Fergusons about our relationship when Marlene approached Jim and me in the garage one day, telling us she could see we were spending a lot of time together, flat out asking us if we were having sex. We both denied having sex, telling her we did enjoy spending time together, but that was all.

Marlene said, "That better be all because I think Mom is getting suspicious of you two being around each other all the time."

Marlene's warning did not faze Jim and me as we continued seeing each other, trying to be more discreet. It was obvious that we were not fooling anyone when Mom began giving me her silent treatment. Typically, when

Mom was upset with any of us kids, she would reprimand us if needed. Most times, she would just ignore us until we would approach her to ask if she was upset with us, apologizing for whatever slight she thought we were guilty of. I was content with our charades because not talking to Mom allowed Jim and me to continue seeing each other while Mom continued to collect her checks, which is probably why she did not confront us.

My foster siblings had figured out that Jim and I were "boyfriend and girlfriend," teasing me about liking an older dude, telling me they would keep our secret because they thought Jim and I were both "cool people." Still, I feared that they might slip and accidentally say something to Mom and Dad, which would cause the end of our relationship, with Jim possibly getting in trouble, or more likely, I would be kicked out of the house. So I kept a low profile with my siblings by not talking about Jim, instead choosing to tell Roxanne everything about our relationship.

I was lucky to have my best friend by my side. Roxanne alleviated a lot of stress for me because she was a good listener who did not judge me for my actions. I needed to share the details of my relationship with Jim with someone I could trust. Roxanne was my person. I needed her input to make sure I was not imagining Jim's love for me or my love for him and to make sure I was not simply infatuated with the idea of sneaking around with an older guy. Of course, Roxanne's first piece of advice was to tell me that Jim was too old for me, and she thought I should go on a couple of dates with guys my own age.

"There are a couple of guys at school who have been crushing on you for a while. Why not go out with them, have some fun, see how you feel about openly dating someone your own age instead of being in a relationship that requires you to sneak around all the time? If Jim is 'the one,' it will not hurt your relationship if you go out on some dates."

Jim and I had never discussed being exclusive, so I took Roxanne's advice and went on a couple of dates with two guys. My first date was with a friendly, cute junior football player whom I had crushed on in previous classes we had together; he was still in love with his cheerleader girlfriend, who had recently broken up with him. I did not mind that I was probably his rebound. He was funny and kind, and we had a good time for a couple of weeks. Of course, the football player got back with the cheerleader, which hurt my feelings, mostly because I felt like he may have used me to make his ex-girlfriend jealous, but who was I to judge since I was often thinking about when I could be with Jim?

My other dates were with Bob, who became a good friend and confidant. I enjoyed being around Bob; he was funny and always up for doing anything. We laughed and talked a lot, often having deep conversations about our futures. Bob was a great guy who had lots of friends because of his fun personality. I enjoyed our friendship, which would continue beyond high school, with me introducing Bob to Jim for a work opportunity.

Jim and I never talked about dating other people. We were content together in our secret space mentally and physically, not leaving much room for others to enter. I knew he had gone on a few dates with a neighbor who lived one street over from Van Ruiten, so I did not feel that it was necessary to tell him about my dating adventures. Our frequency of seeing each other briefly lessened as I ventured away to hang with friends, going to the movies and attending parties. Taking this time to enjoy my friends outside of school was something I had been neglecting because I had been focused on going to school, working, and spending every free moment with Jim.

Spending more time with my friends made me realize I had missed them. I had missed going to dances, to parties, where we would laugh and gossip, all the things high school girls typically enjoy. I made a conscious commitment to myself to balance the available time I had after school and work with friends and Jim.

Panic

Somewhere midsummer, I had missed two periods. All I could think of was Jim's admonition: "If you get pregnant, we are done. We're over." I was scared. I did not want to tell Jim I had missed my period because I did not want our relationship to end, so I called Roxanne and tried not to panic.

Roxanne calmed me down, suggesting that I was not pregnant, that I probably just missed my period because of some hormonal imbalance, telling me to not worry until the next month. "If you do not have a period next month, then you will have to decide what you want to do."

I avoided being with Jim that month, making various excuses if he wanted to get together. Then the worst-case scenario happened—I did not get my period for a second month.

Pregnancy test kits were not available in drugstores in 1973, so I had to go to a doctor or a free clinic for testing. I had no way of going to a private physician without asking Mom to take me, so I asked Roxanne if she would take the bus ride with me into Los Angeles to the closest free clinic to go get a pregnancy test. We made plans to go the following Saturday. The few days passed very slowly, waiting for Saturday to arrive. I left early in the morning, telling Mom I was going to help Roxanne paint her room, so I would be gone all day.

The bus ride to Los Angeles was stressful as I ran through the what-ifs of my possible pregnancy. I was naive about the process of having an abortion. Would I have to stay in a hospital? Would I need permission from my guardians? Should I tell Jim before making any decision? Still, I knew I would not tell Jim since he had so adamantly told me that our relationship would end if I got pregnant. I was on my own with this decision. I was lucky to have my friend with me for support.

I sobbed when the doctor told me I was pregnant. The thought of being a teenage mother was overwhelming. The thought of Jim possibly going to jail for statutory rape if I did not have an abortion was unacceptable. I was too young and obviously too irresponsible to have a baby, so I had the D and C procedure done that day.

The legalization of abortion had just occurred in January 1973, when the U.S. Supreme Court ruled to protect a woman's right to have an abortion without government interference (*Roe v. Wade*). I was very fortunate to have been able to seek support for my decision in a safe clinic environment, a decision that was not easy for me to make but nevertheless would have happened legally or illegally.

Initially, the procedure was no worse than getting a pap smear. Then the severe cramping kicked in, making it difficult to hold back the uncontrollable stream of tears—tears from the painful cramps, tears of sadness, hoping that my body was not damaged for when the time would come that I would want to have a baby, tears for stupidly thinking the "pull out" birth control method would work, tears of frustration because I could not tell Jim what I was going through, fearing he would end our relationship, along with angry tears, thinking about how unfair it was that I had to go through this procedure without having Jim by my side. Nonetheless, this was my decision to make, and I made the decision alone.

I was so lucky to have Roxanne by my side, supporting me after the D and C procedure, staying with me at the clinic for the few hours that I had to stay in the exam room to ensure there was no excessive bleeding. The bus ride back to Roxanne's house was the longest ride of my life. I was exhausted, trying not to cry, scared that I might start bleeding heavily again during the bus ride. I just leaned on Roxanne, wishing there was a way for me to disappear in a dark room that could hide me from the world. I was so thankful that I could sleep at her house that night to recover physically and mentally.

In hindsight, Jim's warning—"If you get pregnant, we are done"—was very selfish. If I had not been a lovesick teenager at the time, I would have recognized his statement as a character flaw; he was putting the full responsibility of birth control on me, with him taking no responsibility for his involvement. Instead, I accepted that birth control was my responsibility, suffering silently for years, wondering if I would be able to get pregnant, having had an abortion.

Fortunately, I had the distraction of a new job to help me forget the outcome of my pregnancy scare. I had started working mornings immediately after the school year ended in the traffic department at the Bellflower Courthouse from Monday to Friday. The courthouse was a straight shot down Woodruff Avenue, an easy bike ride back and forth. My job was opening envelopes to separate money from parking tickets for processing as paid fines, the good old days when people paid with cash or checks. There were a few times when I thought about sneaking some of the cash money into my pockets to save to buy lunch for myself or save for new clothes, but I was afraid that I would be arrested, and I did not want to have a bad record, possibly preventing me from getting future job opportunities. My previous interactions with police after getting caught stealing had left an indelible impression on me. I wanted to avoid any future trips to the police station.

I did not mind working through the summer to save money. I hoped I would be able to save enough to buy a used car before starting my junior year in high school. Jim told me that he would help me find an inexpensive car that might need some work, promising to do whatever repairs were necessary so I would have a safe vehicle. Until then, my bike would be my only means of transportation to work.

I enjoyed riding my bike the two miles from home to the courthouse. There was not as much traffic as there is today, making an outdoor bike ride a serene event. I was concentrating on the cadence of my legs powering the pedals, challenging myself to pedal faster, imagining that my legs were powerful pistons, pushing me into the wind that kept my face cool and my hair blown back out of my face. I would challenge my endurance by working up to a faster speed that would shorten my time on the one-and-a-half-mile flat straightaway of Woodruff Avenue.

Sex Offender

One morning my serene bike ride was disrupted by an intruder. I could sense a car driving slowly behind me. At first, I thought it was going slowly to turn into an apartment complex driveway that was just ahead of me, so I pedaled a little faster, but the car stayed with me, eventually driving up alongside of me. I looked over to see a male driver through the open passenger window. He was the only person in the car.

He was smiling at me when he said, "Good morning. You look like you are working hard pedaling that bike. Would you like a ride?"

I replied, "No, thanks. I'm fine with riding my bike." I pedaled faster.

I thought he was going to drive away when he pulled ahead of me, but then he slowed down again to let me catch up. Seeing the car slow down caused an adrenaline surge in my body. I knew something was not right about this situation, but I dismissed my thoughts, thinking that I was safe because there were cars passing in the other lane.

As I caught up to the car, I glanced over at the driver, who was smiling when he said, "You are so pretty. Look what you've done to me."

I do not know why I looked, but I did. I looked down to see what he was referring to. My stomach was knotted, my heart started racing, and fear set in when I saw that his pants were unzipped and he was masturbating with one hand, his other hand on the steering wheel as he drove slowly next to me.

Oh no, oh no, I thought. *This cannot be happening.* Tears began to flow down my cheeks as I pedaled as fast as I could to get away from his car, but he would only speed up again to stay next to my bicycle.

"Are you sure you don't want to put your bike in my car to take a ride with me?"

I did not answer him. I did not look at him. There was no one walking on the sidewalks whom I could stop to ask for help. I did not want to turn into the next apartment complex, fearing that he might somehow overtake me if no one were around, so the only thing I could do was pedal as fast as I could to the liquor store ahead, where I often stopped for a soda. They knew me there. They would help me. I tried not to cry, telling myself to keep pedaling fast, to remember everything about his car, what he looked like, focus on the details, just keep pedaling.

I couldn't help but sob. I was so *scared*. I could barely breathe as I pedaled for what I felt in that moment was my life. In my head, I was screaming, *Why do these things keep happening to me? What am I doing that makes men want to do these things to me?* The fear and helplessness that were surging throughout my entire body brought me back to those moments when I could hear my father entering my bedroom, knowing he was going to hurt me, knowing there was nothing I could do to stop the pain.

Not this time, I told myself, pedaling so fast and hard that my lungs started to hurt. *This time, I will escape. This time, I will fight as hard as I can. This man will not overtake me, even if I have to ride my bike into the oncoming cars on Woodruff Avenue.*

The man in the car did not follow me into the liquor store parking lot. I threw my bike on the ground, running into the store as fast as I could, sobbing, yelling, "Call the police! Please call the police! A man followed me here in his car. The license plate number is . . ."

I described the car, telling the store owner that the driver of the car had exposed himself to me while driving alongside me on Woodruff Avenue, masturbating. Then I slumped to the floor, sobbing, waiting for the police to arrive. Now that I was safe, my body was free to release the terror, which kept coming in tears. I could not stop crying. I felt like I was going to vomit just before the liquor store clerk handed me a damp cloth and a cold can of soda.

"Here. Put this cloth on your face. You look red hot. Sip some of this soda. It will help calm you."

"Thank you," I sputtered between sobs.

I did not realize how thirsty I was until I chugged the entire soda down as soon as the can touched my lips. Drinking that soda did calm me down. I felt safe sitting on the store floor, knowing no one on the outside could see me. While I waited for the police to arrive, I wondered, *Why do men think it is okay to do these sexual things to me? Is there something about me that makes me look like a victim?*

A police car arrived quickly with a male officer who introduced himself. Then he began to ask me questions about what had happened, asking me to describe the man, the car, anything I could tell him to help with identification. When the officer completed his questioning, he asked if I would take a ride in the police car with him to possibly identify the man who had followed me.

"Will he see me?" I asked. "I do not want him to look at me. I do not want to be close to him."

The officer assured me that I would be safe. "You can stay in the police car with me. I will be with you the entire time."

The officer put my bicycle into the trunk of the police car and then drove onto Woodruff Avenue, back the way I had just come, turning into one of the apartment complexes that I rode by on the days I cycled to work. The officer told me that another police officer was in this complex, questioning a man who owned a car that matched the description and license plate I had given to them. He drove to the back of the complex, slowing down in front of an apartment, where another officer was standing, talking to the man who had followed me in his car.

"That's him. The man talking to the police officer is the man who followed me," I said nervously as I slid down into the car seat to avoid being seen. "Please keep driving. I don't want him to see me."

The police officer assured me that everything was going to be okay. "You're safe. You did good. You do not need to worry about that man harming you or anyone else."

The man who followed me, the man I was able to identify, was a rapist, a rapist who had just been released from prison a few months prior to this incident. He was arrested as soon as I identified him and returned to jail to await a hearing for indecent exposure and, I assume, violating parole. I was called to be a witness for the state at his court hearing. Fortunately, he was removed from the courtroom when I was called by the judge to testify.

The questioning was humiliating and embarrassing as I had to answer questions about his penis: "Was he erect or flaccid? Which hand did he use? Were his pants pulled down or just unzipped? Did he ejaculate? Did he have any birthmarks? Were there any identifiable marks on his penis? What color were the pants he was wearing? What did he say to you when he was masturbating?"—so many questions about the penis, about the act.

At the time, I wondered why it was necessary for the victim to provide such a detailed description of the genitalia. I thought that identifying the offender should be sufficient. Still, as uncomfortable and embarrassing as it was for me to testify in court in front of a judge, an attorney, and police officers, with my social worker by my side, I gathered the courage to make it through the process.

Testifying in court helped me move away from my mindset that I must be doing something wrong, something that made me a target for sex offenders. Testifying helped me understand that I was the victim. It was not my fault. Testifying was a cathartic experience. I felt empowered knowing that my eyewitness testimony allowed law enforcement to put a rapist back in prison.

Chapter Four

Marriage Proposal

On my sixteenth birthday in June 1973, Jim presented me with a card.

"Don't open it just yet. I need to tell you some things. When I noticed you were away from home a lot, having a good time, it made me sad that you were having a good time without me. I am embarrassed to say I was even a bit jealous, thinking about you dating other guys, but I promised to give you space to explore your options. I need you to know that I love you and I have missed you. Now go ahead and open the card."

I laughed teasingly. "How do I know this is for me? My name isn't even on the envelope."

Jim replied, "Oh, it's for you, only you."

The front of the card said, "Without you . . . the days are long . . ."

The inside of the card said, "The nights even longer."

At the bottom of the card, Jim had written two words: "Marry me?"

I felt the tears welling in my eyes. "Really?" I exclaimed. "You want to marry me?"

"Yes," he replied. "I want to make us official so we can stop sneaking around. I want to spend the rest of my life with you."

"Have you told Mom and Dad yet?"

"No, I wanted to hear your answer first. So will you? Will you marry me?"

Through happy tears, I said, "Yes, yes, I will marry you!"

We drove to the beach to spend the afternoon making plans for our future. The first task was to tell Mom and Dad, which we agreed to do that evening. Jim asked me if I would prefer to have our own house to move into as soon as we were married instead of spending money on a honeymoon.

"Of course," I said. "Having our own house would be the best wedding present, but how are we going to get the money to buy a house?"

Jim told me that he had some money saved and that he would work more hours with Dad. The possibility of having our own home—living in our own space together without having to share with others, me never having to worry about acclimating in another foster home—was the greatest gift I could ever wish to have. A home that would be ours meant more to me than having a big wedding or a honeymoon.

Through tears, I replied, "Yes, yes. I would love to move into a house that belongs to you and me. I cannot think of a better wedding gift."

Jim put his hands on my shoulders, looking at me intently as he asked, "What do you think about graduating from high school a year early so we can get married next summer? I don't want to wait two years to marry you. I want to be in our home together by next year."

"How am I going to graduate from school one year early?"

"I think you can take extra classes to move up your graduation date. Do you want to graduate early?"

"Well, yeah. If we are planning to have our own house to move into as soon as we get married, I would think that we both need to be working."

Jim suggested that I check out my graduation options with my school counselor. "You focus on completing the classes you need to graduate high school this year. I will focus on finding a home for us. We also need to recruit Marlene to help us with the wedding plans so we can be married and living in our own home by this time next year."

We headed home just before dinnertime, excited to share our news with Mom and Dad but also worried about how they were going to take the news of our relationship. More importantly, how were they going to feel about our decision to get married?

I told Jim that he was going to have to be the one to explain our relationship and our desire to get married to Mom and Dad. "Mom and Dad are your parents, not mine. I do not expect Mom to be very happy when she finds out that you and I have been romantically involved."

"Mom doesn't need to know every detail about our relationship. Let's keep it simple. We will explain to them that the more we hung out together in the garage, the better we got to know each other, becoming friends first.

Besides, I think Dad will be thrilled. I think you are his favorite kid in the house after the brothers."

"Yeah, Dad likes me as a foster kid living under his roof. I hope he still likes me as much when he finds out his son wants to marry me."

"Don't worry. I will handle my parents. Everything is going to be okay."

The closer we got to the Van Ruiten house, the more nervous I became, thinking about what reaction Mom was going to have when she learned of our relationship. I also tried not to think about the worst-case scenario, which would be both Mom and Dad being angry with Jim and then taking steps to have me removed from their home.

When we drove up to the house, we could see Mom and Dad through the louvered windows sitting at the kitchen table. At least we weren't going to have to rouse them from their bedrooms back into the kitchen to talk. I was so nervous and scared, I almost asked Jim if he would mind breaking our news to his parents by himself, but I knew that it would be better to face them now than later.

Jim and I entered the house through the front door, turning right into the kitchen. Dad looked up at us, not saying a word.

Mom turned around in her chair, looking at us inquisitively, asking, "Is everything okay?" I am sure she was wondering why Jim and I were entering the kitchen together.

Jim replied, "Yup. Everything is okay. In fact, everything is better than okay. Joannes and I have some good news to tell you."

Neither Jim or I moved to sit at the kitchen table with Mom and Dad, instead standing in the center of the kitchen, backed away from the table, as if we were preparing to give a presentation. I preferred to stand because I was too nervous to sit, also feeling that it would be presumptuous of me to think that just because their son loved me, I would suddenly be allowed to join Mom and Dad at their dinner table. We foster kids had never held a place at the Ferguson family dinner table.

As expected, Mom was not pleased to hear about the friendship Jim and I happily described to her and Dad. She *tsk*-ed when Jim would emphasize that our friendship evolved as we bonded over music, spending more time together, learning more about each other. I doubt that Mom believed our relationship was platonic.

She looked at me with what I felt was anger and some disgust, saying, "What's done is done. The two of you have already made your decision. It does not matter what Dad or I think about it. I just want to know one thing. Did either of you think about the trouble your relationship could cause for me and your dad? If social services found out Joannes, a minor, was spending time alone with you, an adult male, in our house, they would have surely stripped us of our state license. The two of you are damn selfish, if you ask me, thinking only about yourselves instead of thinking about how your actions could affect everyone in this house!"

Jim said, "Mom, I would never do anything to jeopardize you and Dad. Joannes and I were just friends, hanging out. We did not have any intentions to become romantically involved. It just happened. We truly love each other. I have asked Joannes to marry me."

Dad finally spoke. "The two of you are going to get married?"

Jim replied, "Yes, Dad. Joannes has said yes to marrying me."

"Well, good for you two. You must be meant for each other since you are both willing to risk so much, including being kicked out of this house."

Jim asked Dad, "Are you going to kick us out of the house?"

Dad replied, "No, I'm just pointing out that you must really be in love to jeopardize so much to be with Joannes. I'm happy for both of you."

I started to cry. I always felt that Dad had love for me. He was a man of few words. In this moment, his words meant the world to me.

I turned to Mom. "I'm sorry, Mom. I'm sorry we did not stop to think about the consequences, but Jim and I love each other. I appreciate everything you and Dad have done for me. It would break my heart if our actions hurt you in any way. I hope you are not mad at me."

Mom replied, "Does it matter if I am upset with you? What's done is done. I just wish the two of you had thought about the consequences of your actions before getting this far along in your relationship. Now sit down and tell us what your plan is from here."

Jim and I pulled out chairs from the kitchen table to sit with Mom and Dad, sharing our plans to get married in June. We talked about my plan to take extra classes so I could graduate from high school in June, a couple of weeks before our wedding, allowing me to get a job to help out with the expenses we expected to have for the house that Jim planned to buy for us instead of taking a honeymoon.

The excitement of getting married began to wane when Mom told us that I would need my parents' permission to get married because I was a minor. California state law required that both parents must give parental consent for a minor to get married. Even though I was in a foster home, my mother and father still had parental rights until I turned eighteen, a fact that made me furious because I did not want to ask my father for anything. I did not want to communicate with him at all.

Getting my parents' permission was going to be the most difficult task for me because I did not know if my mother was still with my father; nor did I know where either of them were living, I had not been in contact with my parents for two years. The joy I had been feeling when I thought about marrying Jim was quickly displaced with dread and fear as I flashed back on the abuse I had endured by my father.

I told Jim that I would not ask my father for anything, even if it meant delaying our marriage until I was eighteen years old. I still had not found the courage to tell Jim that my father raped me, so he was confused when I insisted with some anger in my voice and tears in my eyes that I wanted no contact with my father.

Jim put his arms around me. "I'm sorry that the thought of seeing your father is upsetting you this much. I get that you might be worried about him hurting you, but you should know I would never let anyone harm you. Your father will no longer be able to harm you because I am with you. I will protect you."

Jim suggested that he be the one to contact my father. "I can talk to your father alone. You do not have to be there. All you need to do is contact your social worker to find out where your parents are, and I will do the rest. Besides, I want to ask for their permission to marry you. They are still your parents, and you may feel differently about them someday. More importantly, we have to talk to your father to find out where your mother is living. You want your mother and sister at our wedding, right?"

"Yes. I want my mother and sister at my wedding, but I do not want my father anywhere near me."

I understood why Jim wanted to ask both of my parents for permission, but it scared me. I could not help but feel that Jim communicating with my father would somehow allow him back into my life. I did not want my father to think that I wanted to speak to him or see him. The last thing I wanted was for my father to think that I wanted him involved in my life.

Jim had no idea of the extent of abuse I had suffered by my father, and because I was not brave enough to tell him, I had to finally acquiesce, telling Jim that I would ask Mom to help me contact my social worker. I assumed that there was a social worker assigned to me even though I had not seen or spoken to anyone at social services since I had moved into the

Fergusons' home. It took only one phone call to contact a social worker who told Mom that social services did have an address for my mother and father but not a current telephone number.

Jim decided to write a letter to my parents, giving them some information about himself to let them know how happy we were, how our relationship had developed, bringing us closer together until we eventually fell in love. Jim emphasized, I think more for my benefit and peace of mind, that he would make sure to impress upon my father that he would do everything necessary to protect me from anyone or anything that might cause me harm. Jim closed his letter by asking my father to call him at our house phone number (we did not have cell phones in 1973) to plan a meeting.

As much as I detested the idea of Jim communicating with my father, I held onto the hope that I would be able to see my mother soon, also knowing that my mother had never been able to leave my father when I did live with them, so I knew that there would be no seeing my mother without my father now.

A couple of weeks passed before my father did call Jim, asking to meet face to face at the Van Ruiten house. I was not home when Jim spoke with my father. Knowing that I did not want to see my father, Jim suggested that they meet somewhere away from our house.

My father knew he had the upper hand. "Jim, you tell me you love Marie. I love her too. So it should come as no surprise that I will need to see her in person if I am going to give my permission to allow her to marry you. This is not a frivolous thing you are asking my wife and me to do. I want to see both of you."

Jim asked, "Will Mrs. Boman be coming with you?"

"Unfortunately, my wife will not be with me as she is currently in a convalescent home, recovering from some complications with her paralysis."[6]

"I am sorry to hear that. Are we able to visit Mrs. Boman? Maybe Joannes and I can meet with both of you at the convalescent home."

"I want to meet you with Marie before disturbing my wife."

"I will have to talk to Joannes first before I make that decision for her. What telephone number should I call you at?"

---

6   My mother was in a convalescent home being treated for depression after a recent suicide attempt.

"There is no decision to be made. Either I see Marie in person or I won't give my permission for the two of you to get married."

Jim told my father that he would have to call him back after speaking with me about meeting. When Jim told me about his conversation with my father, I cried.

"Sounds like we are going to have to wait until I turn eighteen to get married because I cannot bring myself to ask my father for anything. This is so typical of him, trying to control and manipulate every situation for his personal benefit."

Jim, looking at me with exasperation, asked what the big deal was about seeing my father for a short amount of time. "I know he hit you. I know he hurt you and your mother. I understand why you don't want to see him, but maybe he has changed. Maybe he is ready to apologize. Can you forget about the bad things he's done for this short amount of time, just long enough for him to give us his signed permission for us to get married?"

Jim's words infuriated me. How could he think that being harmed by my father was something easily forgotten? How could he think that an apology would magically make the pain and anger of physical abuse disappear?

Sobbing, I looked at Jim and said, "No, you can't understand because what you don't know is that my father raped me! My father hurt me many times. He will never change. His apology would mean nothing to me, and I never want to see him. I don't even want to ask him for anything, even if it means delaying our marriage. I want nothing to do with my father!"

I ran into my bedroom, falling onto my bed, sobbing in frustration, anger, and dread. I was dreading what Jim would think of me now that he knew my truth. I just knew that he was going to think less of me, either because I had been raped or because I had not told him sooner.

Jim followed me into my room, approaching me to put his arms around me. "Oh no, Joannes. I am so sorry. I am sorry. Why didn't you tell me this before? I wish you had told me. I'm sorry I pushed you to reach out to your father. I'm sorry."

I moved into Jim's arms, my body shuddering with sobs. "I couldn't tell you because I thought you would think less of me because of what my father did to me. I thought you would look at me differently. I did not tell you because I was afraid of losing you. I was afraid you would not love me anymore."

Jim replied, "I'm not going anywhere. You are stuck with me now. I'm not going anywhere without you."

Fear Returns

Jim and I decided to contact social services again to ask them to locate my mother. I told my social worker that I was still fearful of my father and that I did not trust his motivation when he insisted on seeing me before he would tell me where my mother was living. I was also concerned about the health and safety of my mother, not trusting that my father was telling the truth about her living in a convalescent facility. Fortunately, my social worker thought that my request was reasonable and agreed to get back to me as soon as she confirmed my mother's location.

About a week later, I was at home, watching television, when I heard yelling coming from the front of the house. As I walked down the hallway toward the kitchen, I heard Jim talking to someone. The other voice sounded familiar to me but did not register until I looked out the front louvered windows to see my father standing at the end of the driveway, yelling at Jim. I stopped at the kitchen table, my body frozen with fear, tears welling in my eyes. *No, no. Why is he here? How did he know where to find me?*

As soon as I saw that it was my father standing outside of the Van Ruiten house, my body reacted as if I was back in my bedroom, watching my father approaching through the darkness, the same fear building inside of me in the form of a vise grip, squeezing the breath out of me at the pit of my stomach.

I ran back down the hallway to see if anyone else was home. Fortunately, one of my foster brothers was in his bedroom. As soon as he saw me crying, he jumped up from his bed, running to me to ask if I was okay. Sobbing, I managed to tell him that my father was in the front yard and that it looked like he and Jim were going to have a fight.

"Stay here," he said as he ran to the front of the house.

Marlene, hearing me yell, had come out of her bedroom to ask what was going on. I told her the same thing. Then the two of us ran into the kitchen to see what was happening outside. My foster brother was standing next to Jim in the driveway. Jim had a hammer in his hand.

My father was yelling at Jim, telling him that he wanted to see me. "I'm not leaving here until I see my daughter!"

Jim told my father that he was not going to allow him to see me in his drunken state.

This made my father angrier. "Allow me? You won't allow me to see my daughter! Here's a news flash for you. I can take Marie home whenever I want. She is only here because her mother and I agreed to *let* her move into foster care. How do you think I got this address? I can take her home anytime I choose."

Jim said, "That may be the case, but as long as I am standing here, you are not going see your daughter unless she wants to see you or if you are accompanied by someone from social services."

My father started to approach Jim with a look I was very familiar with, the look of anger building up to physical altercation, the same look he would get before hitting my mother or grabbing me to hit me with a belt or his hand.

I knew that the guys would be able to handle my father, but I did not want to chance having the police show up because of a brawl in our front yard, so I ran to the front door, yelling through the screen at my father, "Here I am. Why are you here? How did you find out where I live?"

My father replied in his condescending, manipulative manner, "Oh, it's Marie. Hi, Marie. How nice of you to grace us with your presence. Is this exciting for you, seeing all this commotion for you?"

"You're the one causing the commotion. I did not ask you to come here."

"Oh, my brave Marie, trying to be so grown up, wanting to get married so Jim can take care of you yet too stupid to realize you won't be getting married anytime soon because I am not going to give my permission."

I resisted, responding to my father with anger when he said I was "too stupid." I was very familiar with his condescending tone baiting me to engage in our old pattern, with me crying or screaming in anger or frustration as he laughed at me, making fun of my frustration and tears, often saying, "Poor Marie. Have I hurt your feelings?" My father's tactics to engage me had worked when we lived in the same house because I had nowhere to escape his abuse. Now my confidence was high with the support of people who cared about me holding their ground against my father.

"Oh, I realize you are not going to give your permission because you still think you can control my life, but I can wait until I turn eighteen to get married. I would rather wait than ask you to do anything for me. In fact, I would prefer you had nothing to do with me or for me for the rest of my life."

My father started to walk toward the front door. "Marie, why don't you step outside to talk to me? Come tell your father to my face how smart and independent you are now."

Jim quickly stepped in front of my father. "Do not walk any closer to the front door. You need to leave now."

My father, clearly agitated because he could not have control over me, yelled at Jim, "I'm sure you love my daughter! She is quite the charmer, but don't you fucking tell me when I should leave. I came here to talk to my daughter and you about your upcoming marriage. Now that I'm here, you want me to leave?"

My father tried to take a different path toward the front door, but the guys cut him off, telling my father to stop where he was.

I screamed at him to just go away. "I don't need anything from you!" I was so angry that my father still had the power to make me feel afraid and uncomfortable, I turned and ran back to my bedroom, with Marlene following to sit with me until I calmed down.

Later, Jim told me that he was able to calm my father down, convincing him that he should leave because getting the police involved would not be good for anybody. He told me that my father tried a few times to convince Jim to encourage me to come out and talk to him, but Jim told my father that today was probably not a good time for that because of my father's altered state.

Jim was able to establish enough rapport with my father to convince him to give Jim the address and telephone number for the facility where my mom was living. As happy as I was to hear this news, I know that the only reason my father gave the information to Jim was to ingratiate himself for what he hoped would be another opportunity to meet. I'm sure that my father knew there was no way of getting to me without having Jim's support.

I would not have to worry about my father's interference in my upcoming marriage plans or his attendance at our wedding because he continued his history of drunk driving citations and arrests for drug possession, theft, and carrying a firearm without a license, all culminating in his arrest and sentencing for armed robbery of a Long Beach bar with a friend as his accomplice. My father began serving a two-year sentence in September 1973 at the Tracy California State Prison.

Bittersweet Reunion

My mother was living less than ten miles from the Van Ruiten house at Lynwood Convalescent Home. It was astounding that she could be so close to me yet no one from Social Services told her or I about each other's location. I guess it was up to me to tell my social worker that I wanted to see my mother and sister but I never thought to ask if it was possible to see them without my father, I expected my mother to attempt to find me after I was placed in foster care.

I ignorantly thought there was communication between social workers and parents to encourage counseling to affect change. I thought assistance would be provided for my mother to get her the support needed to bring me back home with her and my sister. What I did not think about is that my mother had to ask for help, she had to want to change her circumstances to have me come back home. If I was honest with myself, I knew my mother did not have the strength or willpower to do anything other than what my father asked of her.

I wondered if my mother even cared where I was living. I wanted to believe that she missed me yet seeing how easy it was for my father to find me made me feel she did not care or maybe she did not attempt to find me to keep my father away from me.

Any feelings of abandonment I felt about my mother were momentarily replaced with sadness for her having to live in this dank, depressing facility blanketed in the smell of urine and other unidentifiable odors surrounded by others in various stages of lethargy. I spotted her sitting in a wheelchair barely able to hold herself upright looking into the distance her face expressionless. I had witnessed my mother in various stages of depression but today was different she seemed heavily sedated. I learned that she had been living in this convalescent home for the past year receiving treatment for her depression after another suicide attempt it seemed that treatment was simply a daily regimen of drug therapy without counseling. Come to think of it, I do not recall a time or any mention of my mother ever getting regular psychiatric care for her depression only drug treatments which seemed to me to be futile, especially when living with my father.

It made me happy to see my mother's lifeless body perk up when she spotted me walking toward her after I had exclaimed, "Mom, it's Marie. I found you!" I watched as she looked at me with what seemed to be disbelief then ever so slowly her beautiful smile broke through not quite as big and vibrant as I remembered but enough to make me smile through tears as I watched her spirit break through.

I was surprised at my tears. I had forgotten how much I loved my mother. I had buried my love for her and my sister to accept and successfully transition away from my family to make a new life for myself in foster care. Allowing myself the luxury of hope, hope that my mother would someday be able to provide a home for me and my sister without my father, hope was not realistic because she was unable to take care of herself.

I hugged and kissed my mother's forehead before kneeling down on the floor in front of her looking into her eyes, "I have missed you mom. I'm happy to see you are okay."

"Marie, where have you been?" my mother asked.

"Mom, what do mean where have I been? I've been living in a foster home since you saw me last, the foster home I live in now is very close to here and is also where I met Jim. Mom, Jim is my fiancée his parents run the foster home I live in now."

"Your fiancée you're going to get married?"

"Yes mom, we will talk about that but I want to know more about what happened to you after I was placed in foster care. Did you ever try to find me? Where's Faith?"

"I guess I've lost track of time. I thought you might be living on your own by now. Your father never told me where you were living, I guess I thought you would contact us when you were ready. Things got worse with your father after you left, he was drinking more, taking drugs, always fighting with me and beating on Faith. She was put in a foster home too. I don't know where she is."

How easily my mother said, "I don't know where she is." Her eldest daughter was living in foster care now her youngest daughter was also gone[7]

---

7 My sister was in and out of foster homes until she returned to live with both of my parents when our father was released from prison in 1975.

yet she seemed so complacent as if having your children taken away from you was a normal parental occurrence.

I wanted to ask my mother why she never tried to visit me. I wanted to ask her why she had not tried to contact Social Services to find out where I had been placed. I felt she didn't care enough about me to find me, I had to keep reminding myself she was probably in survival mode with no emotional capacity left to think about her children, or was I overestimating her love for us, maybe she enjoyed the party lifestyle that surrounded her when she lived with my father.

Yet as I looked at my mother, a shell of herself, she was the literal example of a person who had been beat down, exhausted from the continuous battles fought with my father. I wanted to be angry with her for not trying harder to get away from my father, not only for herself, but for my sister and I, I wanted to resent her for her lack of complacency when she spoke of my sister and I being in foster homes yet I could not bring myself to blame my mother because she too had suffered so much from staying with my father. I felt sorry for her because she was not strong enough to live without my father and I felt sadness for her because she was so sad but did not seem to know what to do to help herself.

"Mom, you can contact Social Services to find out where Faith is living. You, and unfortunately dad still have parental rights, including knowing where we live. Your parental rights is one of the reasons I am here today. Jim and I want to get married in June."

"Get married? How are you going to get married you're too young."

"Well, that's one of the reasons I wanted to find you. I need your permission to get married because Jim and I want to get married next June but before we talk anymore about me getting married, I want to know why you are in this convalescent home?"

"I tried to overdose with pills again, I just could not take living with your father anymore. Faith had to be put in foster care because I could not take care of her and your father was always too high or drunk always beating on me. I gave up. I was just not strong enough to keep living."

"Mom, you are strong enough to keep living just not with dad. He is never going to change. What are your plans when you get out of here?"

"I don't know. I'm thinking I might ask my sister if Faith and I can come live with her in Texas she's been trying to get me to move back to Texas for a while."

"Then you should move to Texas. You need to break away from dad to live where you can be safe and happy. Jim and I will help you in any way we can."

"I'll see," she replied.

My mother's response was disappointing but I checked my aggravation reminding myself she was depressed and unsure of her future. Jim and I kept the rest of our visit lighthearted catching my mother up on my journey to Van Ruiten, my foster siblings and how I was doing in school.

Jim eventually pulled his chair in close to my mother taking her hands in his; "Mrs. Boman, will you give your permission for me to marry your daughter? It would make us very happy to get married as soon as she graduates with our honeymoon celebration to follow when we move into our own house, something I know your daughter wants more than anything, to live in her own home."

My mother said she would give her permission for Jim and me to get married but she had one condition "you have to buy me a new dress to wear to your wedding." I laughed as I knelt down in front of my mother, "Mom, of course we will buy you a new dress, new shoes, whatever you want the mother of the bride has to look her best for the wedding photographs. I will take you shopping as soon as you are able."

Now that the hurdle of getting consent to be married was resolved Jim and I could finally feel excited about moving forward with our wedding plans. Jim focused on helping dad close more contracts to increase their workload of remodeling jobs to earn as much money as possible to insure we would have a down payment for a house to move into as soon as we were married. My focus would be to complete high school and to continue working at the courthouse saving all the money I made to contribute toward our wedding.

I never doubted we would have a house to move into as soon as we were married because I believed Jim when he told me he would make it happen by working harder. I knew he was motivated to move out of his parent's house yet I had very little knowledge of the financial requirements to make a house purchase. I blissfully looked forward to living in a house I could call my home, a home where I would be safe, a home were Jim and I would build our life together to live happily ever after.

Wedding Plans

On a weekend in September Jim asked if I wanted to go shopping with him, "Shopping, your least favorite thing to do, what do you want to go shopping for?" I asked.

"I've been thinking I asked you to marry me without giving you an engagement ring. I thought we should go to Zales Jewelers today to look at wedding rings, maybe we can find a set with a nice diamond ring for you to wear as an engagement ring. What do you think?"

Feeling sassy I replied, "Well, duh what girl would say no to shopping for jewelry, so yes, please take me shopping for my engagement ring so that I may show it off."

When I decided on a 1 ct. solitaire princess cut diamond set in yellow gold Jim surprised me when he got down on one knee in the Zales store to put the ring on my finger again asking, "Will you marry me?" I replied, "My answer is still yes." Jim kept the matching gold band to place on my finger on our wedding day. It would take me about a week before I tired of frequently looking at my hand to make sure the ring was still on my finger seeing a diamond ring on my hand was a wonderful daily reminder that I would soon be married living a happy life with Jim in our own home.

Having an engagement ring on my finger inspired me to begin making plans for our wedding, our first task was to recruit Marlene, who told me she was too old to be a bridesmaid but would love to plan our wedding reception to be hosted at the Van Ruiten house.

Jim already knew who his groomsmen were going to be, I needed to select my bridesmaids so I could have my girlfriends with me to help me make a wedding dress decision. The friends I would choose to participate in my wedding were not only special to me but also generous because they would have to pay for their own dresses, typically expected of bridesmaids yet I worried about my high school friends wanting to spend money on a dress for a wedding.

I asked Roxanne to be my maid-of-honor. I felt my friendship with Roxanne had deepened as we enjoyed our many summer adventures together maintaining that closeness into our high school years, while time with other friends had lessened as we shifted to different activities spending less time with each other. Once I made the decision for Roxanne to be my maid-of-honor it was easy to complete my bridesmaid ensemble with three of my closest high school friends.

I felt loved and great happiness when my friends said yes to participating in my wedding, in that moment I recognized how wonderful my time at BHS had been surrounded by many kind and fun friends. School provided me with normalcy, in school I was not a foster child, I was just me, I was just like all the other kids attending high school looking forward to graduating someday.

In early December I made my first layaway payment on my wedding dress, a white Victorian beaded high-collared neckline with sheer lace long sleeves and double layered satin with a lace overlay floor length skirt and white beaded headband with flowing sheer tulle with a March deadline to pay in full. My dress was quite elaborate for a summer wedding, my bridal team even suggested the dress might be too hot for a late June wedding, of course my teenage mind was not thinking about practicality I wanted the most beautiful dress I could afford.

The baby blue bridesmaid dresses with floppy white hats and the groomsmen tuxedos, also baby blue, reminded me of a light blue sky filled with white clouds representing a new day, a new life. Only blue skies ahead.

My mother who had been moved to a group home associated with the Lynwood Convalescent Home arranged to take my mother shopping for her dress. My mother told me she thought I might forget about shopping with her since I had only called her once and had not returned to visit her. I was guilty of being self-absorbed in my quest to get married. Even though I loved my mother I was also guilty of avoiding visits with her because seeing my mother brought back the sad memories, the memories of what my life used to be when I lived with my parents. I wanted to avoid thinking about those times, I wanted to avoid thinking about my mother choosing to stay with my father instead of choosing me. I did want to share my happy life event with my mother but I also wanted to keep her at a distance until I was sure she wanted to participate in my life without my father ever being present.

Junior/Senior Year

I got to school early the first day of my junior year so I could go to the administration offices before class to tell Mr. Sienknecht, Mrs. Hodge and Mrs. Garrison about my June wedding plans. I wanted to make sure they left June 22 open to attend my wedding. Of course, they were surprised to hear about wedding plans because I had not told them anything about my relationship with Jim as always, Mrs. Hodge and Mrs. Garrison were very happy for me as was Mr. Sienknecht who took the time to ask me to sit with him in his office where he listened intently as I told him about my love story with Jim.

As always Mr. Sienknecht was insightful, "I am not going to say you are too young to get married because I know you have probably heard those same words from others who also care about you. I am only going to wish the best for you and Jim because it sounds like both of you have put a lot of thought into your decision and your future life together. I also know how determined you are and am confident you will succeed at anything, including marriage because that is what you want. You have always applied yourself to achieve your goals. I am selfishly disappointed that this will be the last year we have together but I will look forward to seeing you at graduation and attending your wedding in June."

Walking to class I realized how much I was going to miss seeing Mr. Sienknecht on a regular basis, he had been my safe harbor, I knew I could talk to him about anything and he would listen without judgement. I found myself wishing I had spent more time with him but I was busy doing what he encouraged me to do thriving in school.

My final year of high school would be a challenge but I was motivated to achieve the reward of my wedding day shortly after graduation day. Fortunately, senior year was more about graduation activities than having a full curriculum, I would only need to complete two college courses in addition to my six high school classes before my June 13 graduation date.

I enrolled in two evening classes at Cerritos College, Elements of Nutrition and Interior Decoration, classes I thought would be fun and easy while also helping to prepare me for being a good homemaker. Reality check, college courses were more difficult than high school and Interior Decoration was more design theory than how to make the inside of my house look cute. The subject matter was not as fun as I had hoped but I pushed through knowing I would soon be done with school.

Roxanne convinced me to take Auto Mechanic class with her so we could be in a class together in my final year of high school she thought we should learn basic maintenance for the used cars we both planned have by mid-year. We were the only girls in the class which motivated Roxanne and I to meticulously complete the class project so that we could get the only A grade to be awarded for the fastest, timed reassembly of our automobile combustion engine with carburetor, spark plugs, piston, and timing belt. Roxanne and I were not the fastest to reassemble and start our engine but we did complete the task coming in third out of seven teams with a B grade and bragging rights for being the only girls in a class filled with boys.

The time I spent with Roxanne in Auto Mechanic class was bittersweet as the realization set in that this would be our last year of high school together. Roxanne had been a good example of confidence tackling whatever she wanted to accomplish methodically and calmly, participating in in this class full of boys highlighted our shared competitiveness and drive, our team project was a memorable culmination to our time spent together in high school a friendship that would definitely continue after graduation.

House Hunting

A few months before our wedding dad surprised Jim and I when he handed Jim an envelope that contained $18,000 in cash to be used as a down payment for a house.

As dad placed the envelope in Jim's hand he said, "I've been putting small amounts of cash away for a while for emergencies. Your mother and I have everything we need so I want to help you with the purchase of a house. This is between you and me do not tell your mother I gave you this money." Dad winked at me, I put my arms around him thanking him for his generosity and support of our marriage.

I had always admired dad's strong work ethic, he seemed to enjoy his work yet I never had a sense of how well his business was doing. It was a big deal that dad was giving us this much money. I could not help wondering if Jim and I were worthy of such generosity based on the years Jim had been so rude to dad, while I felt dad had given me so much already by being a kind, supportive foster parent.

Dad was, and still is the most authentic example of a loving, strong man whose actions spoke a thousand words. I can still manifest him sitting at the kitchen table in the Van Ruiten house giving me a wink and a smile letting me know he *saw* me. No words were necessary, I just knew dad was there if I needed him. He became the father I always wished I could have.

Dad did have one condition for the monetary gift, "I want to be involved in helping you select a house so I can help you inspect the structure and foundation."

Dad's one condition was also a gift, who wouldn't want an experienced General Contractor around to help with the selection of your home. And so, Jim and dad began the search for our house as I bowed out of the process leaving it to the construction experts, to find us a good home. I needed to stay focused on school and coordinating wedding reception details with Marlene.

High School Graduation — June 13, 1974

As the school year progressed, I would often find myself in deep thought wondering if graduating early had been the best decision for me as I began to feel sad thinking about missing my friends and missing the opportunity to graduate with my classmates. Some of my pensiveness developed as I took a lot of light-hearted joking from my guy friends who liked to tease me about choosing an older guy to marry instead of giving them a chance, while my girlfriends would ask why I did not want to wait one more year to get married.

I began to second guess my decision to graduate high school early, realizing I had not put a lot of thought into how much it would mean to me to graduate with my senior classmates.

Jim was so anxious to move out of his parent's house then I got swept up in our wedding plans not giving much thought to how much I would miss the experience of graduating with my closest friends.

Instead of regretting my decision, I decided to feel thankful, recognizing that everything about my high school years had been a positive experience, my counselor, my friends, my teachers, my classes, extracurricular activities, everything about my time spent at BHS had been the most satisfying experience of my life up to this point, an experience I would often look back on with fond memories.

So, even though I did not graduate with my friends from the class of '75 I did graduate with the class of '74 celebrating at a fun all-nighter at Disneyland with friends and my fiancée.

Wedding Day — June 22, 1974

"The first day of our life together..." aptly printed on the front of our wedding invitations.

I was hopeful and excited looking forward to this day of ceremony and celebration that was the beginning of the next phase of my life, a life that I knew would be filled with love and happiness.

The first person I looked for as I walked down the church aisle following our five-year-old ring bearer, and ten-year-old flower girl my arm locked with dad was my mother who looked lovely in her floor length peach colored dress and gold-toned flats with her long black wavy hair falling on her shoulders waiting to give me away. Jim and I had asked my mother if she would like to be the one to give me away, we wanted her to feel she was an important part of our ceremony, she loved the idea and dad was content to walk me down the aisle to deliver me to my mother.

My mother's big, beautiful smile was like a beam pulling me back in time when it was just her and I together when she would smile, and I would smile back at her content in her presence. It made me very happy that she was able to share this important milestone of my life seeing her dressed up and happy in the moment was the best wedding present she could give to me.

Mom Ferguson looked as happy as she could with a slight twinkle in her eyes and a thin smile that always seemed to have a hint of mischief lingering at the corners. I know she was not thrilled that her son was marrying a foster teenager but she loved her son so she tolerated me which did not hurt my feelings because I knew it was more about her than me.

My bridesmaids, my best friends, all looking lovely smiling at me sneaking in a thumbs-up reminding me of how lucky I was to have their genuine friendships. They looked fresh and cool in their short-sleeved dresses on this warm summer day unlike me who could feel the sweat beads forming inside my long-sleeved Victorian wedding dress which looked fabulous.

I smiled at Jim who had tears in his eyes looking handsome in his baby blue tuxedo matching his groomsmen, three who had the stereotypical 1970s hippie look of shoulder-length hair a contrast to Jim and his best man who donned shorter ear length haircuts. I had lovingly nicknamed this great group of guys the motley crew because their looks and personalities were so varied.

Dad kissed my cheek as he released my hand for Jim to take into his the two of them shaking hands before dad stepped away to stand next to mom. Jim and I turned toward the minister to commence with the wedding ceremony, which was brief as intended, vowing to love each other for the rest of our lives before turning toward our friends and family to be introduced as Mr. and Mrs. Ferguson. I felt the power of love when Jim took my hand in his to walk out of the church as Mr. and Mrs. Ferguson surrounded by our family and friends all people who loved us, I held on tightly feeling hopeful entering into the next phase of my life.

Jim and I stepped outside into the bright sunlight with big beaming smiles only to be ambushed by a shower of rice thrown at us from all directions. We had to spit out the rice grains that had flown into our mouths because we were laughing so hard, for a minute. Jim had to yell at the motley crew to cease so we could open our eyes, silly guys. My bridesmaids helped me pick the rice grains out of my hair before we stepped back into the church with the photographer for wedding pictures.

Thankfully, our wedding party was small which allowed us to wrap up the photo session quickly. Ron took the wheel of our getaway car, mom's Monte Carlo, driving me, Jim and Roxanne to the Van Ruiten house to celebrate at the reception Marlene had planned and coordinated with the help of our neighbors.

As we approached the Van Ruiten house, I could see family and friends lined up in two lines from the street curb to the front door of the house waiting to greet us. I was overwhelmed with tears of joy having a brief moment of recognition for how much my life had changed since I first arrived at the Fergusons home a scared, anxious fourteen -year- old girl with no idea of what the future had in store for her, to now, married and looking forward to starting the next phase of my life with Jim by my side.

The path to the front door was a slow walk as we were hugged and high-fived by friends, we were enjoying the love but desperately needed a glass of water as the heat of this summer day had left us dehydrated. Roxanne ran ahead into the house to get water for us when she noticed I was literally red-faced, saved by my maid-of-honor. We could always depend on each other.

Jim and I were stopped by the photographer just as we were ready to step into the house, he wanted to take a picture of Jim carrying me over the threshold into the house. Jim told him he would only pick me up in front of the door as if he were going to carry me over the threshold but would not cross because he would be carrying me over the threshold of *our* home soon. Jim picked me up, the photographer snapped a few photos then, thankfully, we stepped into the house on Van Ruiten to begin celebrating with our family and friends.

Marlene had anticipated the limited house space not accommodating forty people and had decorated tables with umbrellas set up in the backyard by the pool, as well as tables in the living room set close to the buffet that was set up in the kitchen. (having that kitchen at the very front of the house finally came in handy.) I don't recall sitting down to eat, I did make sure my mother and sister were sitting with mom, dad, and Marlene while Jim and I mingled among our guests.

Time passed quickly as we accepted well-wishes while trying to get to each guest to thank them individually for coming to our wedding. I was looking for Mr. Seinknecht when I saw Mrs. Hodge and Mrs. Garrison, I broke away from other guests to go to them, to thank them for coming. I was disappointed when they told me Mr. Seinknecht was unable to come because of a family matter. They handed me an envelope he had asked them to give to me. I read his card the next day which was filled with kind words and wonderful wishes for me and Jim, there was a generous gift enclosed. When I finished reading the card, I felt the final chapter of my high school experience had ended.

When we finally sat down to open gifts, I realized I was parched, I had to gulp down more water before Jim and I raised our cold glasses of champagne to be toasted by our family and friends. I had Jim move a chair closer to me for my mother to sit in so I could interact with her since I had been unable to spend much time with her until now.

After all the wedding gifts had been opened Jim stood up and handed me a small box with only a bow on it, "I want you to open this box. What is inside this box is the reason I did not want to carry you over this threshold." "Who is this gift from?" I asked. "Just open it," Jim said.

Inside the box was a key. Puzzled, I looked at Jim then I looked at the key again. It had the word Kwikset on it which I thought was usually a house key.

"Is this a house key?" I asked.

He said, "Yes, it is our house key. We will be going home to our own house tonight."

"What? Really?" I was stunned. I could not believe what I was hearing. Everyone started to clap and cheer as I stood looking at Jim then looking at the key in my hand. I felt like I was in a dream.

Forever Home

After the guests were gone and arrangements were made to get my mother and sister back home, I raced to change out of my wedding dress into a more comfortable dress to sit with Jim, dad, mom and Marlene to talk about the day and thank each of them for everything they did to help make our wedding a memorable event. It was surreal for me to be sitting with the Ferguson family as a member of the family, instead of a foster kid. I was married to their son. I was their daughter-in-law; I was a sister-in-law. It felt good to be an official member of the Ferguson family.

I was ecstatic thinking about Jim and I moving into our own house, he teased me saying he was surprised I waited so long before finally asking him to tell me about our house. Jim told me he had found a "nice little fixer-upper house" for us in Bellflower just two miles from the Van Ruiten house. He had put a good faith deposit on the house pleading with the real estate agent to let Jim borrow a key so he could surprise me on our wedding night.

And so, it came to be…Jim and I left the Van Ruiten house to drive to the house that would be our home. Crossing over the threshold into our home Jim said, "welcome to your home, Mrs. Ferguson," leaning in to kiss me taking my hand to guide me to our bedroom where he had laid out sleeping bags with pillows and Coleman lanterns for lighting.

We undressed to snuggle together in the sleeping bags to talk about how we were going to remodel our house to include a big family room to hang out with our kids that we planned to have in five years, and dogs which I wanted right away to guard our large backyard. We planned to add more bedrooms and a large garage with lots of workspace for Jim to organize his tools for his construction projects. We talked about our future plans until we fell asleep snuggled together on the floor.

As I drifted off to sleep, I thanked whoever was listening for guiding me to my forever home.[8]

---

8   Our home was on Blaine Ave in Bellflower only one block from the Junior High School I attended when I was placed in the Fergusons foster home. Full circle?